NEW
Directions
for HOLY
Questions

Progressive Christian Theology
for Families

Claire Brown & Anita Peebles

Illustrations by Perry Hodgkins Jones

Morehouse Publishing
NEW YORK

*To our readers and all wonderers, may you have curiosity
and courage to explore new directions for your holy questions.*

Morehouse Publishing, 19 East 34th Street, New York, NY 10016
Morehouse Publishing is an imprint of Church Publishing Incorporated.

Cover design by Jennifer Kopec, 2Pug Design
Interior design and typesetting by Beth Oberholtzer

A record of this book is available from the Library of Congress.

ISBN-13: 978-1-64065-455-6 (paperback)
ISBN-13: 978-1-64065-456-3 (ebook)

Contents

Introduction for Kids

Dear Readers (those young in age and young at heart),

We are so glad you are here, holding this book. We welcome you to this journey of asking some big questions about God the same way we start the first chapter: You are beloved. Beginning, middle, and end. Each chapter begins with a question. Some questions are about God, some are about Jesus, some are about the church and the Bible and rituals that Christ followers do together. Some questions have answers. Some are simple, and some are complex. And some questions help us learn about ourselves more than we learn about an answer. There are all sorts of questions in this book. We invite you to add your own questions to these, too! You might think "Why?" or "How?" or "I wonder . . ." As you read, journal or color or talk about these questions with someone you love. Be curious!

In the middle of each chapter, you will find some spiritual practices. A spiritual practice is an activity that helps you come close to God's heart and feel God's presence. There are lots of different kinds of spiritual practices in this book: some that you can do by yourself and some that you can do with other people. We encourage you to try all of them and listen to your heart for what works best for you.

Toward the end of each chapter are stories about justice. These stories tell how individuals and groups have worked to make the world more generous, loving, and safe for all people. As you read these justice stories, think about what you can do to make the world a better place.

Who are we, the writers? We are beloved children of God, too. We are women who were called by God to be pastors and to serve God's church, especially children and youth like you! We are friends who like to sit on porches and drink tea and laugh and cry and sing and dance and learn together. We are curious people who love Jesus and who want to learn all we can about how to live with justice in this world.

As you read this book and ask questions and wonder, we pray that you will know in your bones and in your breath and in your heart that God loves you just the way you are. We are praying for you, as are the generations that have gone before us that we call the clouds of witnesses. You are not alone, for you are held in the love of the Holy all your life.

Beloved child of God, this book is for you.

Wondering with you,
Claire and Anita

Introduction for Adults

A couple of years ago, Claire's family made the unfortunate backyard discovery of a small nest of baby rabbits that had died. Her then four-year-old was distraught and wanted a bunny funeral. As a mom and an Episcopal priest, she felt like this was a great learning moment. Ritual! Meaning making! Reverence for all creation! Grief and acceptance! All was going well until, several hours after the "service," her son said, "Can we go check and see if God has raised the bunnies from the dead yet?"

Uh oh. That was not quite right. Why does it feel so difficult to have these conversations? How do we ponder big, holy questions with kids in a way that helps us all grow?

Parents and professional practitioners who care about sharing the Christian faith with their kids can run into all sorts of sticky spots and weird ideas as we explore the big questions. This book is not full of answers or a template that will smooth a bumpy conversation, but it's meant to be a companion in your conversations as you and the children in your life learn, grow, and wonder together. More advanced readers might pick this book up on their own, and that is awesome! We encourage adults to let those learners lead the conversation. Others might benefit from reading aloud one chapter at a time with an adult and having some encouragement and guidance in their learning. Each chapter also includes a few summary points that offer adults a script for emerging questions about God and faith with children not old enough to read this book on their own.

We are companions on this journey with you. Claire is an Episcopal parish priest raising two young children with her spouse in southeast Tennessee. Anita is an ordained Baptist pastor associated with the Alliance of Baptists, and works with children and youth in Seattle, Washington. We met while students at Vanderbilt Divinity School in Nashville, where we studied, prayed, served, and worshipped with people with diverse theologies.

In each chapter, we retell a story from the Bible. All acts of translating ancient texts make editorial choices, and we believe that it can be faithful and helpful to tell these stories in fresh ways and with accessible language. With every retelling, the scripture reference is included. We encourage you to look up these passages in your preferred translation and dig deeper into the context and content of the story and surrounding passages of scripture. This continued exploration is also a great way to help children understand the complexity and breadth of the Bible and see where else curiosity might lead.

Anytime we study and read and pray with the Bible and theology, we will run into questions. Sometimes questioning faith is scary or lonely, and it can feel like you're the only one wondering. Let us say here and now that you are not alone! Asking questions is one way to love God with your mind, by growing deeper in your understanding of Holy Presence in our world. As you read this book, remember that these questions are great! In fact, *New Directions for Holy Questions* is filled with open-ended questions on purpose. We hope they offer reflection and conversation between children or children and adults. Many of these questions don't have one answer and are meant to expand the readers' curiosity about scripture, theology, prayer, and our experiences of God. Maybe you will find new ideas here that are different from what you've learned at church, or new ways of thinking about a certain Bible story. Maybe you aren't satisfied with the open questions. If you find yourself asking these questions in your own faith, we encourage you to check out the faith formation resources for adults on our book's website, newdirectionsforholyquestions.com.

This book covers a lot of territory, asking and exploring many of the core questions that have shaped Christian faith and theology for thousands of years. Our ambitious hope was to offer insights, instruction, and continued reflection around the biggest theological doctrines and ponderings of our religion. Yet it is just one start, or one point of continuation, in a lifelong journey of holy curiosity and learning. None of these questions come with one definitive answer, and the chapters are not meant to reach tidy conclusions. In our seminary new-student orientations, faculty and administrators repeated versions of this refrain: "You will not learn answers here. You will learn to ask better questions." The journey of faith doesn't look like mastering handwriting, memorizing multiplication tables, or remembering to say "please" and "thank you." This is an ongoing learning, getting to know ourselves, our rich and complex tradition, and God, that is never concluded. Maybe *New Directions to Holy Questions* will offer some answers, some insights into important questions of faith, but we hope, most of all, that it leads you to richer and more interesting questions as you grow in the knowledge and love of God.

The prompts for spiritual practices in this book are meant to require little to no preparation and be adaptable for all ages. Some involve mindfulness and body-based breath practice, others incorporate spiritual attention into daily routine, and there are also simple activities with art reflections, going on a walk, or connecting with friends and neighbors. You might make colored pencils, markers or crayons, and paper available for art responses. With these practices, there is no "right" way to do them. The only guidance we can offer is that you make space to experience the Sacred with you, wherever you are and whoever you are with.

Prayer for the Journey

Dear God, give us grace and peace as we love the children you have
*   entrusted into our care.*
Protect and nourish them body, mind, and soul:
That they would know you delight in them, in all of who they are and who
*   they are becoming as they grow;*
that they would know they are enough and beautiful and know how to love
*   themselves;*
that they would be deeply kind in an unkind world;
that they would find belonging and know their worthiness;
that they would survive and flourish in a world that isn't designed for them
*   to live;*
that they would always remember the good news that you love them just
*   the way they are;*
that they would know they are deeply beloved, by you and by others;

and that they would live and move and have their being in you, knowing
you in their mind but also finding your presence and guidance in all their
emotions and experiences;

that they would be nurtured into just who they already are, not who we
think they should be;

and that they would be so surrounded by loving community that they take
that sense of welcome and belonging everywhere they go, extending
it to others.

Be with us each day, reminding us of your faithful presence, deep
compassion, radical love, and boundless grace.

In the name of all that is holy to each and every one of us,

Amen.

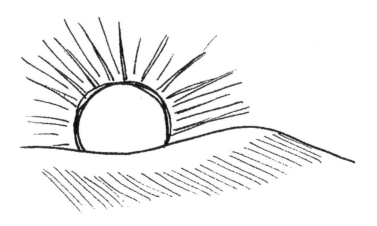

1
Who Am I?

Long, long ago, as the stories say, before there were people and homes and cities and roads, before there were dogs and books and trees, there was only the earth, with a spring of water in it. God took some dirt from the earth and formed the first person with the dirt. Then God breathed on the dirt person, and they came to life. God made a lovely garden, full of all kinds of beautiful plants and foods, and put the first person there to take care of the garden and enjoy it. God didn't want the first person to be lonely, so God created many kinds of animals, too, and the person loved the animals and gave them names. God decided to make another person as well, so that the first one would have a partner and helper. So the two human beings lived together and cared for each other as they tended the garden and loved the animals. (Retold from Genesis 2)

In the beginning of everything, Something Holy hovered over the chaotic waters. Then the Something Holy spoke, and became God. The words God spoke called into Being the dark and the light, the earth and the sky, the land and the water. God said, "All of this is sacred. All of this is good." Next, God spoke the words that created Life, animals with fins for the water and animals with wings for the sky and animals for the land that crept, slithered, trotted, and hopped. There was a place for every living thing, and growing things for every living thing to eat. God said, "All of this is sacred. All of this is good." Then God said the words to make Being alive, and there was a Human. God created the Human to be an echo of God on the earth. "The Human will take care of all this beautiful Creation. All of it is sacred. All of it is good." Because God created everything from Something Holy, every Created thing is sacred. (Retold from Genesis 1)

upendo

Liebe

الحبّ

爱

AMOR

प्यार

ЛЮБОВь

amour

love

אהבה

uthando

αγάπη

You are beloved. Beginning, middle, and end. From the moment your heart began beating, through the joys and pains of growing up, until the time when you, like all of us, return to God, God loves you. When God created you, God blessed you and made you to live and love. God delights in you being yourself, in all the complex and full and wonderful you-ness. No one else is like you in the whole entire world.

Every person is beautiful and beloved. Diversity is what makes our world so wonderful. People with dark and medium and light and freckled and spotted skin. People who speak Xhosa and Spanish and Hebrew and Arabic and English and Russian and more. People with small and tall and wide and narrow and curvy body shapes. People who use wheelchairs and crutches and who run and who lie down and who dance. All races, ethnicities, abilities, languages, body sizes, etc. Every person is as valuable as anyone else. None of us are better or worse than anyone else.

Spiritual Practice: **Give thanks for your body, heart, and mind. Pray through your body, from the top of your head to the bottom of your feet. Say, "Thank you, God, for my [body part] that can [perform an action that the body part does]." Remember to give thanks for how you love when you reach your heart and for all the unique ideas that are all yours when you reach your head.**

Every single person who has ever been born is a part of God's family. Sometimes we talk about church as a family, or as "the body of Christ." Like the parts of a body (in 1 Corinthians 12, for example), every part of a family has a special purpose and plays a unique role in making life beautiful. That's the same for humanity. Every person is an expert in their own lives. You, as an individual, know the most about what it is like to be

you! And you have gifts and talents that are all your own. Even when you don't feel very special, that doesn't change that you were created to be only yourself by a loving and imaginative Creator.

What is something you appreciate about yourself? How do you want to grow? Who do you want to be?

Justice Story ~ *In 2011, Sonya Renee Taylor posted a picture of herself on social media, stating that she was proud of her body and loved her body. For a large Black woman, that was an act of resistance. Soon, thousands of people all over the world were sharing photos of themselves, sending affirmation to each other, and a community called The Body Is Not an Apology was born. This organization shares resources for people seeking to embrace their bodies as they are, to push back against narratives of body shaming, and to uplift people of all different identities. Today, The Body Is Not an Apology continues to educate and encourage people on the journey of loving and seeking justice for all bodies in each of their particular shapes, colors, sizes, and abilities. All bodies are good bodies.*

Spiritual Practice: **Find some mud after a rain or near a body of water or make mud in your yard by mixing soil and water. Make the mud really squishy. (If you don't have mud, find some clay or Play-Doh). Try making figures of people out of the mud. As you make the figures, remember that God created humans out of the soil from the ground, like clay.**

When you are done with the figures, leave them outside. Remember that humans live on earth for just a little while compared to the whole life span of Creation. God's time is not our time. Remember that God is continuing to create newness every single day.

Being human is complicated. It can be confusing. It is often messy. We have bodies that need food, water, shelter, and safety. We have hearts that thrive by giving and receiving love. We have a wide range of emotions that help us respond to events in our lives and in the world. Most humans need to be in a community of people, like a miniature family of God. When we are part of a community, we can remind each other of how much we are loved, because sometimes we forget. People can even know God through a community of people, in how individuals love each other and care for the earth and advocate for justice. Because each of us was created with a little bit of the Something Holy inside us, part of being human is to look for that holy in each other and to live so that others can find the holy in us.

Who is in your community? Who helps you learn how to live and love? Who sees God in you?

The stories in the Bible tell us how God wants to be in relationship with God's people. These stories can help us understand parts of who we are as humans and how we can relate to God, to the Creation, and to each other. When we read the Bible, we can find words of love and encouragement that help us be our best selves. We can also know, through our experiences of living every day, that God is present with us and reminding us that we are beloved. You were created to love and be loved.

For younger children

SAY: Every person in the world is a beautiful, beloved part of God's family. God created you because God loves you. God created you to love and be loved.

DO: Make mud or clay figures. Be amazed that God created you and that you can create, too!

PRAY: God, thank you for making me and loving me. I am amazing, and you did a great job! Amen.

2
Who Is God?

Long ago, God's people, the people of Israel, were forced to become slaves in Egypt. They worked without pay or protection. God saw the people's suffering and loved them and called someone to help lead them to freedom. His name was Moses. One day he was out caring for sheep in the wilderness when he saw a bush that was on fire, but not burning up. How strange! When he went to look more closely, a voice called to Moses and told him to take off his shoes in reverence. The voice said, "I am the God of your parents, the God of Abraham and Sarah and Hagar, the God of Isaac and Rebecca, and the God of Jacob and Leah and Rachel." The voice went on to give instructions to go and speak to Egypt's king and lead the people to freedom. Moses was worried. "What if the people don't believe me? Who do I tell them has sent me?" God answered, "I am who I am. Tell the people 'I am' sent you." (Retold from Exodus 3)

Since the beginning of time, people have had many different understandings of God. People in all cultures, times, and places have had a sense of something or someone bigger or more powerful than humans. Some think of God as a parent; others think of God as a judge. Some believe God is mysterious and hard to describe; others think of God as being very clearly understood and defined. Some people think that God is far away from us; others believe that God is everywhere, working in the world and present all around us, as close as our breath.

What do you imagine when you think of God? What does God look like? Sound like? What names do you call God?

It's hard to find words or names for God that fully describe what we mean or what we experience with God. Maybe that is why when God and Moses were talking, God offered the name "I am." I am? What does that mean? Calling God "I am" is like calling God "God is here." In their journey to freedom through strange places and difficult times, the people knew that God, "I am," was always with them.

The God who talked with Moses, the God of Abraham and Sarah and Hagar, the God of Isaac and Rebecca, and the God of Jacob and Leah and Rachel, is the God of the Jewish faith as well as the Christian faith. Christianity teaches that God is one, that God is loving and good, that God is mysterious, and that God is near us and at work in our lives and in the whole world.

Some people call God Father or Mother. Some people imagine God by picturing nature, like a rock, a fire, or a wind. Some people think of God as a warrior, and others know God as a peacemaker. Some people call God their friend, their doctor, their shepherd, or their home. All these names are in the Bible and are ways that Christian and Jewish communities might talk about God. One way of naming God might work for you for a while, and then later you use a different name.

Spiritual Practice: **What is a name for God that you think is beautiful and true? Write about or draw a picture of how you imagine God. Or draw images of those names as a way of praying and celebrating all the ways that people can know God.**

When we share our ideas and images and names for God with each other, we bring together pieces of a beautiful picture and understand God more clearly.

Spiritual Practice: **Find someone that you can ask about their ideas, names, and images of God. Share your writing or drawing with them, too.**

Are any of your ideas, names, or images for God the same? What new ideas, names, and images did you learn from them?

Jesus, whom Christians believe is God's special child, reminded his friends of the old teaching that the two most important things that people can do is love God and love one another.

We love God in many ways through our many stories, names, and images of God. We show our love for God through prayer, worship, caring for creation, and by growing, flourishing, and being our whole selves.

We also love God by caring for other people. Care for others takes many different forms and happens in many different parts of our lives. When we care for others, we are expressing God's love for them and loving God at the same time. We care for people individually, like our friends and neighbors and family. We also care for others when we make the world more just and fairer, more peaceful and loving for everyone.

Justice Story ~ **Sometimes people describe working for justice, peace, and love in our world as a "movement." That word doesn't mean just moving your body or a physical motion, but also moving attitudes and ideas to work together, and moving people's hearts to care for one another. Movements for good change in the world need lots of people and lots of different perspectives to grow and make a difference. The #BlackLivesMatter movement began in 2013 after a Black teenager, Trayvon Martin, was killed by a white man who simply thought Trayvon didn't belong in his neighborhood, and the killer did not go to jail. The founders of this movement wanted to affirm the importance of Black lives and flourishing in the face of this horrible crime and the court's decision. But #BlackLivesMatter is not about one person or family, and it is not about the vision of one leader. In fact, the women that started this movement describe the need for many voices and perspectives as a movement that is "leader-full," powerfully guided by many different leaders and strong people. When**

a movement is leader-full, that means that people have worked together to think about a problem and strategize about how to effect change. Through lots of care, education, community building, and planning, leader-full movements empower multiple people to carry out the mission of the movement instead of looking to only one expert person to guide everyone. The #BlackLivesMatter movement is just one example of a movement that seeks to be led by everyday people who are empowered to create change in their communities.

When we share our visions for a better world and work together, and when we share our names and images of God, we are stronger and more beautiful.

What's one way you show your love for God through helping and loving the world?

Jesus teaches us how to love God and love each other. But the idea of a loving God is even older than our Christian religion. We understand God through the ideas and beliefs of the Jewish tradition because Jesus and the earliest Christians were Jewish. In this tradition we find our basic ideas of who God is.

The Hebrew Bible, what some Christians call the Old Testament, tells stories of the beginning of everything, when God created the earth and all living things. God is the Creator, the source of life.

Another key part of the Old Testament is the story of God bringing God's people out of slavery in Egypt to their freedom and new homeland. God is a liberator who brings people to justice and peace.

Throughout the Bible and the experiences of people across time and space, we can find stories of how God's goodness and grace are present to people, no matter what. God is love.

Spiritual Practice: **Spread out and take a big stretch with your body. Close your eyes and think about these three beliefs about God: God is the source of life; God brings freedom; God is love. What images or stories are coming to mind? Use your body, your voice, and your movements to act out these three words: *life; freedom; love.* Your movements can be silly, peaceful, serious, dramatic, or small.**

In the book of Acts in the New Testament, there are many stories about the apostle Paul, who was one of the first Christians and spent his life travelling to church communities to speak about Jesus and encouraging them in their faith. Once, when Paul went to the city of Athens, Greece, he gave a big speech about God and worship. He told the people that God made all things. Paul told them that God wants people to ask questions and look for God in their lives. Finally, he told the people that God is everywhere, that God's love is always with us. "In God," Paul said, "we live and move and have our being."

Where do you live?
God is there with you and all around you.
How do you move?
God is moving with you and giving you the strength to move.
What is your name? What is your favorite thing about yourself?
God loves you, knows you, and celebrates your being, your self.

For younger children

SAY: People talk and think about God in many ways and use different names for God. It can be hard to describe God because God is so big and beautiful and strange to us, but we know that God always gives life, freedom, and love.

DO: Draw a picture of how you imagine God.

PRAY: God, you are love; God, you are freedom; God, you are life. Amen.

3
Who Is Jesus?

Jesus was part of David and Bathsheba's family, who were part of Abraham and Sarah's family, who were part of God's family . . . (*Retold from Matthew 1*)

The angel Gabriel went to bring God's word to a girl named Mary. Gabriel said, "I bring greetings to you from God. God loves you and is choosing you for a special purpose." Mary was confused. What kind of purpose would God have for her? The angel told Mary, "You will become pregnant with a special child. You will name him Jesus. He will be a great leader and teach the world about how to live in the kingdom of God." Mary wondered, "How can this be?" Then Gabriel said, "Mary, nothing is impossible with God." Bravely, Mary replied, "Here I am, ready to answer God's call." (*Retold from Luke 1*)

When the Emperor Caesar Augustus called for a count to be made of all the people in the Roman Empire, everyone went to their hometown to be counted. Joseph the carpenter went from Nazareth in Galilee to Bethlehem, the town of King David because he was part of David's family. Joseph brought Mary, the woman he was going to marry. She was pregnant with a miraculous child . . . (Retold from Luke 2)

Jesus was a person, like you and me. He was born, he grew, and he died, like all humans. But that wasn't the end of his story. Jesus was a part of God's big family. Jesus was God's special child.

Spiritual Practice: **Think about a time when you saw the sky full of stars. Do you know any of the shapes made by stars, called constellations? In Genesis 15, God tells Abraham that a great family will be made from all of Abraham's descendants. God says that one day there will be as many people in the family as stars in the sky! When you look at the stars, remember that millions of people over thousands of years have also looked at the stars and found themselves part of that great family.**

Long before Jesus was born, Hebrew prophets spoke for God to the people. They saw the injustice in their communities, how the poor people got poorer even as the rich people got richer. People were without homes and food and were sick, while others dined at lavish banquets and hoarded their wealth. The prophets were sad and angry because that's not how God wanted God's people to live. God wanted the people to care for each other and live justly. The prophets told the people to

change their hearts and lives. They also said that one day a liberator would come to help them, a person who would be known as the Messiah, the chosen one of God, and that person would end all injustice. The prophets didn't know when or where that person would come, but they encouraged the people to have faith in God's justice.

What is a prophet? Who do you know who speaks for God? Who have you heard described as a prophet?

When Jesus was born in the city of Bethlehem, some people began to wonder if he was the Messiah. Those people started to look for other signs in Jesus's life that he was the Messiah. When he was young, his parents Mary and Joseph, the carpenter, traveled back to Nazareth, where they lived. As Jesus grew up, his parents raised him in the Jewish tradition, including going to Jerusalem to worship at the Temple (Luke 2:41–52). Jesus's family wasn't rich or well-educated; they were working class. Jesus probably followed in Joseph's footsteps as he grew up, learning the carpenter's trade.

When Jesus was around 30 years old, he was baptized in the Jordan River by his cousin John the Baptist (Matthew 3:13–17). After his baptism, he called 12 disciples to travel with him and spread the good news

about God's love and justice to people all around the region of Judea. The disciples were a mismatched bunch of people, some of whom were unpopular fishermen and tax collectors and lawyers and regular folk. Jesus preached about the kingdom of God and healed people and restored them to their community. Soon more people began to follow him: women and men, old and young, and everyone in between. Jesus and his disciples traveled from place to place teaching about God and doing miraculous works. They didn't carry money and didn't have a lot of possessions, but they worked together and relied on each other. Wherever they traveled, people offered them hospitality.

What do you think it was like to travel with Jesus? Why did Jesus call all sorts of different people to be his disciples? How do you

imagine people offered hospitality to Jesus and the disciples?

One of Jesus's most famous teachings is called the Sermon on the Mount. Many people gathered to listen to him as he told them about the kingdom of God and blessed them. He said, "Blessed are you. You who feel sad, you who desire justice, you who feel small. You who are kind, you who have brave hearts, you who are peacemakers. All of you are blessed, and the kingdom of heaven will welcome you." (Retold from Luke 6)

Jesus told the people they were light for the world, and they should brighten the world with their gifts to bring justice to all. He told them they were like salt that brings out the best flavor in any dish, and that they should lift each other's well-being and encourage each other in their community. He even told the people they wouldn't be popular all the time, and in fact some people would not like what they were doing if they followed Jesus. But Jesus told them that they should stay peaceful, be generous, and share God's wide-open love with everyone.

How do others share God's love with you?
How do you share God's expansive love?

Some of the people who thought Jesus was the Messiah were confused. The prophets had described a Messiah who was a powerful warrior and who could bring the mighty down from their thrones. Jesus wasn't a king or a warrior like they had ever seen before. He certainly could do miraculous things, like when he fed over 5,000 people with two loaves of bread and five fish (Matthew 14:15–21), or when he brought his friend Lazarus back from the dead (John 11). They watched as he ministered all over the region of Judea, filled with wonder at how he showed God's expansive love to all people.

What do you wonder about Jesus's life on earth?
What do you imagine he was like?
How would you have felt as one of Jesus's disciples?

Not all the people who paid attention to Jesus were admirers, though. Some of the people were frustrated and challenged by what Jesus was saying. These people plotted together to get Jesus arrested so that they could ruin his ministry. They wanted to remind the people of Judea that the Empire was in charge, and that their way of life was the best. Jesus was arrested. He was put on trial. Eventually, he was killed.

Some of the women who followed Jesus stayed nearby as Jesus died, even visiting his tomb after his burial. The women found that Jesus's body was not in the tomb, but that he was alive again!

After he rose to life again, Jesus appeared to his followers. He prepared them for a time when they would have to continue his work without him. One day, Jesus said goodbye to his disciples and promised that a comforting presence would be with them always, even when he wasn't there in person to work with them. Then he went to be with God. The disciples were sad to lose Jesus again, but they were confident this Comforter would help them continue the ministry that he started.

How do you think the disciples felt when Jesus was arrested and killed?
What did the disciples think when Jesus was alive again?
What actions did Jesus want the disciples to continue with the help of the Comforter?

Over time, even after Jesus went to be with God, people wondered who Jesus really was. They knew he was special, and they knew his followers kept telling stories about him over and over. People began to call him the "Christ," a word that means "anointed one." In those days, only kings were anointed in a special ceremony setting them apart. By calling Jesus the Christ, people recognized that Jesus was an important leader set apart to do God's liberating work.

How can you follow the example of Jesus in your life?
What can you do to encourage others to live according to Jesus's example?

Some people wrote stories about Jesus's life. These stories are called the Gospels and can be found in the beginning of the New Testament. The people who wrote the stories of Jesus's life wanted everyone to know how important Jesus was from the beginning. They told stories about how Jesus Christ was remarkable, from the circumstances of his birth to how he grew up to how he preached and taught people throughout his life. These stories continue to matter to people today. When people decide to try to live like Jesus and follow his teachings about peace, justice, hospitality, generosity, and inclusion, they are called Christians because they follow the Way of Christ that we learn about in the Gospels.

Spiritual Practice: A famous song says, "They'll know we are Christians by our love." Loving our neighbors as ourselves is the best way to follow Jesus. Find a recording of that song that you like and share it with someone you love. You may want to create your own new verses to add to the song! How can you love people as Jesus taught us?

Justice Story — You may already be familiar with Rosa Parks, an African American leader in the Civil Rights Movement. She was part of a movement across the United States to end racial segregation, the unfair and unequal separation of people because of the color of their skin. She is most famous for a moment when she was told to move to the back of a public bus so that a white passenger could have her seat. She said no! This was a brave thing to do because she was arrested for her refusal to give up her seat. Her courage was strong because of her faith in God and her firm belief that Jesus's teachings of nonviolent resistance and change were the most powerful way to

end segregation. She once said, "I would like to be remembered as a person who wanted to be free . . . so other people would be also free." The story of Rosa Parks's work for love and freedom for herself and others reminds us of Jesus's work for love and freedom.

How can you follow Jesus by loving your neighbors?
What would Jesus do if he lived in your city?
What actions show people that you follow the Way of Jesus?

For younger children

SAY: Jesus is God's special child who showed people God's love in a new and powerful way. Jesus lived long ago in Palestine and was a teacher and healer. Jesus died, but God brought him back to life!

DO: Listen to a recording of "They'll Know We Are Christians by Our Love."

PRAY: Dear God, thank you for Jesus and for showing your amazing love in his life. Help me to love like Jesus loves. Amen.

4
Who Is the Holy Spirit?

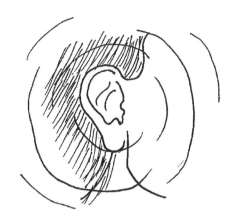

When Jesus was preparing his friends to leave them and go back to God, he promised them that they would not be alone and he would send a Comforter, someone to help them feel brave and peaceful. Jesus ascended to heaven, and as the days passed, Jesus's friends were sad and worried. They had gathered for the Jewish harvest festival, called Shavuot, in Jerusalem, a time when people from all over the world come to worship God.

Suddenly they heard a noise like a loud wind. Something that looked like flames of fire came over the heads of each of Jesus's disciples and friends. They began to speak in all different languages and could tell the story of Jesus so that people from different places and languages could understand. They remembered how Jesus had loved them and taught them, and then they felt brave. They knew that the Comforter had come: the Holy Spirit.
(Retold from Acts 2)

The Holy Spirit is the third person of the Trinity: God the Father, God the Son, and God the Holy Spirit. This is how Christians talk about the way that God lives in and with us all the time. We celebrate the Holy Spirit with us on the feast of Pentecost when Jesus's disciples experienced God's spirit with them. We also understand the Holy Spirit from other places in scripture and from our own experiences. In the story of Jesus's baptism, the Bible describes the Holy Spirit coming down on Jesus while God spoke a blessing over God's child. When we look for God's presence in our lives, we find that God's Holy Spirit comes to us as gentle as a dove, as strong as a wind, as bright as a flame, and as close as our breath.

In the Old Testament, the spirit of God was God's power in the world in creation, speaking to the prophets, and empowering God's people to be strong, brave, and wise. We see God's spirit in the strange and wonderful stories of miracles and in the pillars of fire and cloud that accompanied the Hebrew people out of slavery and to the Promised Land.

What is your favorite Bible story? How is the Holy Spirit in that story?

Like the Pentecost story's strong wind, Christians also think of the Holy Spirit as breath. In the creation poem in Genesis 2, God breathes the breath of life into the first human. The Psalms say that the stars were also made by God's breath, and the letter of 2 Timothy says that scripture is breathed by God. In the Gospel according to John, the Holy Spirit comes to Jesus's disciples when Jesus breathes on his friends. Any time we read about wind or air or breath in the Bible, it brings us back to God the Spirit.

Spiritual Practice: **Practice feeling God's Spirit like breath and air. Put one hand on your belly and one hand over your heart. Take a big deep breath. Do you feel your chest move? Imagine the oxygen that your body needs filling your lungs. The Spirit is God filling us up and giving us life.**

Jesus called the Holy Spirit the Comforter, the one who helps people feel better when they are lonely or frightened or don't know the right thing to do. When we are going through hard times, whenever we are sad or scared or lonely, it is God the Holy Spirit who is right there with us, all the time.

When have you felt lonely or frightened or confused? What happened? How can you remember God is with you the next time you feel that way?

The Bible also talks about the fruits of the Spirit. These fruits aren't grapes and bananas but are ways of living and being with other people that show that God is living in us and guiding us. We can recognize the Holy Spirit's presence and life in people just like we can recognize a plant by the kind of fruit that is growing on it. When God's Holy Spirit is in us, we see love, joy, peace, patience, kindness, goodness, faithfulness, gentleness, and self-control. Those words do sound nice, but what does it mean to show them in our lives?

Love is feeling affection and giving care to others.

Joy is happiness that is bigger and lasts longer than what is happening today.

Peace is a feeling of calm inside us and working to get along with others around us.

Patience is accepting delay or frustration without losing our tempers.

Kindness is putting the needs of others first.

Goodness is making wise choices even when no one is watching.

Faithfulness is trusting that God is with us always.

Gentleness is being careful with other people or creatures.

Self-control is being responsible for how we behave and express our feelings.

Think about these "fruits" of God's Spirit. When do you show those in your life?
When is it hard to do these things? When is it easy?

Justice Story ~ **In Great Britain in 1984–1985, workers in coal mines (a very dangerous job) went on strike. A strike is when workers stop working to try to make their companies treat them fairly. It was a scary time, and a lot of people were angry, tired, and struggling without work. A group of gay and lesbian activists in London wanted to support the miners who were out of work. As people who were often treated badly because of who they loved and how they expressed their identities, they understood how hard it is to be treated unfairly. Their experience encouraged them to want to show kindness and love toward others who were being treated badly and were in need. They formed a group called Lesbians and Gays Support the Miners to raise money to help miners who didn't have enough money and food. Much to their surprise, they became unexpected friends with miners in Wales, and the two very different communities worked together to make**

their communities stronger and more caring. It must have taken a lot of patience and gentleness to have friendship with people from such different backgrounds, but these two communities joyfully worked for each other to be able to live in safety and peace.

Any time we see love, joy, peace, patience, kindness, goodness, faithfulness, gentleness, and self-control, we know and can celebrate that the Holy Spirit is at work in the world.

Spiritual Practice: **Tell a story about a time you've seen the Holy Spirit in people or places around you. When have you been full of love, joy, peace, patience, kindness, goodness, faithfulness, gentleness, or self-control?**

The Holy Spirit is in us, in other people, in beautiful nature and creativity, and in social movements that show those "fruits," and the Holy Spirit connects us to all those people and things like an invisible web. The apostle Paul says that the Creation is waiting to see God's children, and in another place he writes that God's people are as connected to each other as parts of one body. The Psalms talk about conversations between humans, God, and nature. Our connection through the Holy Spirit is also

how we understand that we are connected to people of faith across time and geography, all mysteriously together in God.

Spiritual Practice: **Close your eyes and think about someone you love who is very important to you. Is that person near or far away? Hold out your hand. Imagine that wherever that person is, they have reached out and held your hand. You are connected to them through your holy imagination, through God's Holy Spirit in both of you.**

For younger children

SAY: The Holy Spirit is God's powerful presence in the world and with us every day. When we listen to the Holy Spirit in our minds and hearts, we show God's love and goodness in our lives. The Holy Spirit helps us make good choices and trust God, and it connects us to each other.

DO: Take five big, full breaths, and say, "The Holy Spirit is close to us like our breath."

PRAY: Holy Spirit, be my guide. Holy Spirit, be my comfort. Holy Spirit, live in me. Amen.

5

What Is the Church?

After Jesus was raised to life again, he spent some time visiting with his friends and then went to be with God. His friends and disciples were amazed, confused, excited, and afraid. When God the Holy Spirit came to them, they felt brave and understood that they were called to teach and care for people the way that Jesus did. The church started as a community of people who were putting Jesus's way of love into action: they cared for each other's needs, ate, and prayed together. The church told people the good news that Jesus was alive, and that God's life and love are stronger than death and harm. This led them on all kinds of adventures as they met new people and travelled far and wide to offer care and hope. Like Jesus, the disciples often got into holy trouble with people who didn't like their message of freedom, change, and love. Some were put in jail or hurt. Like the church today, they sometimes made mistakes and had to work hard to be a caring community. But despite their struggles, this little community of Jesus began to grow and grow. (Retold from Acts 1–4)

Spiritual Practice: **What comes to mind when you think of church? Draw a picture or write a description of church.**

Many of us imagine a building where people gather, where we might find pews or Bibles, stained glass windows or crosses. You might think of your church and the memories of worshipping, learning, and being with people you have in that place. You might think about songs or stories you have learned in church.

More than two thousand years ago, the church first began as a group of people who had loved Jesus trying to care for each other and love God. You can read more stories about the first church in the book of Acts. The Christian church was a small group that was often blamed for all kinds of problems. In fact, the name "Christian" was a label from people who didn't like the church very much. Calling these folks "little Christs" was meant to be an insult! But even though many were not happy with this group, many more people were curious and excited about the message of Jesus, and the church grew.

In the 300s, the Roman emperor Constantine made it legal to be a Christian, and the faith became an established religion that spread across all of the Roman Empire, from Northern Africa to Great Britain to Asia. Every small community of the church all over the world has its own character, reflecting the cultures, places, and deepest values of the Christians there. Different churches have different styles and ways of worshipping, different shapes, sizes, and decorations.

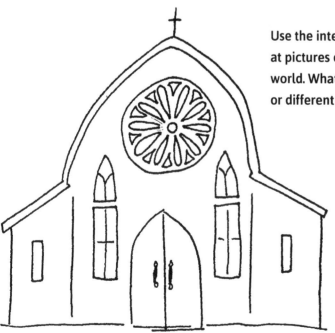

Use the internet or your public library to look at pictures of churches in different parts of the world. What do you notice? How are they alike or different from each other or your church?

The buildings and spaces where Christians gather are very important, special places. They are decorated in the ways that each community believes will best show love for God and help inspire people to think about God, pray, and worship together. They become holy, or special God places because we share special moments of prayer, celebration, sadness, and learning there.

Visit your church or another church in your community.
See if you can visit during the week to look around the space.
What do you notice?

One reason there are so many different Christian churches is because there are different denominations, or groups and traditions that have slightly different beliefs. Those differences might include how a church worships together, the best ways to lead and run the church, or ideas about what it means to live like Jesus and follow his teaching.

While there are differences among us, just like the earliest Christians, the church today is truly all the people who love Jesus, not the place where they gather or the name of their denomination. Anyone who is connected to Jesus in their faith and life is part of the church! Because we love God and follow the way of Jesus, we are all connected to one another in a web of God's love, and that makes us the church.

Spiritual Practice: **Take a piece of paper and draw a circle in the middle. Write "God" or "Jesus" in the circle. Then draw lines stretching out from the circle like the spokes on a wheel or threas of a spider's web. At the end of the first line, draw a picture of yourself or write your name. At the end of each of the other lines, draw a picture or write the name of a different person who loves God: friends and family, saints throughout history, or people from your church. Add as many lines as you want. Your web or map of people attached to one another because of their connections to God is a picture of the church, too!**

Together, we are better at loving God, caring for each other, and caring for creation than we would be on our own. We need the church, other faithful and kind people who follow Jesus, to grow in our connection to God. When the church works together to care for others and creation, living with care and working for justice and peace the way that Jesus showed and taught us, we call that ministry.

Some churches also choose people to serve as ministers in particular roles because they have certain skills and abilities that help the whole community. These people are called pastors, elders, priests, deacons, or ministers, or have another title depending on the church's traditions and practices. They might work for the church as their job or volunteer for certain kinds of work, like preaching, teaching, leading worship, caring for people going through a difficult time, or running the business and building for a church.

Spiritual Practice: **Is there a pastor, elder, priest, deacon, minister, or leader at your church? What is their name? What do they do? Make a card or draw a picture to ask them more about their ministry or to say, "Thank you."**

While these leaders and workers have a particular responsibility in the church, all Christians are ministers. All of us work to bring God's love to the world around us in many different ways. We all can share the good news about Jesus's life and God's love with others. We all can sing and pray to God. We all can offer care and kindness to others and creation because of our love and faith in God.

How are you a minister?

One word we often hear about a church is "sanctuary." This word usually refers to the room in a church where people gather to worship, or a part of that room where an altar might be. Not all churches have a building with a sanctuary, but for those that do, this is a holy place where people meet God. That's why this word is also used to mean "a place of safety." We should be safe from spiritual, physical, and emotional harm all the time, and especially in the place where we meet God.

Justice Story ~ *The idea that people should be safe and free from fear and harm was what started the sanctuary movement in the 1980s. During that time, people from Central America were trying to make a new home in the United States of America and other peaceful places because wars and poverty made their home communities unsafe. When this happens, the person looking for safety can ask another country to take them in, and this is called "asylum" or "sanctuary." Yes, sanctuary like a church! But the laws of the United States were unfairly blocking people from asking for safety, so churches began to work together to offer the sanctuary, the safe space and care that people needed so much. Over 500 churches decided to provide food, money,*  *shelter, and safety for people who needed those things, even if it meant that they were breaking the law. This work of churches offering sanctuary has happened again and again. Recently, Germantown Mennonite Church in Philadelphia, Pennsylvania, provided sanctuary for a woman named Carmela and her children. Because of the church's support, Carmela and her family were able to stay together in the place where they had made their home.*

They knew that the church is not just a building; it is people who love God and love each other, no matter where they are from and no matter how hard or risky it is to show that love.

What's one way that your church works together to show God's love? Ask and learn how you can help with the ministry of loving the world around you!

The church is all people who love Jesus, all Christians, connected by the Holy Spirit. When we connect in our faith as a community, our connection to God grows stronger and is more beautiful.

For younger children

SAY: The church is not just a building or a group of people. The church is everyone who loves and follows Jesus. We are all part of the church, and together we help each other love God and people better.

DO: Make a picture or card to show love to someone in your church community.

PRAY: Dear God, thank you for the church and all your loving people. Help us love like Jesus, together. Amen.

6
What Is the Bible?

Long ago, a young boy named Josiah became king of Judah. During his rule, he ordered that God's temple in Jerusalem should be rebuilt. While the temple was being repaired, a special scroll was found. The scroll held all the instructions for how to read the sacred texts and how to obey God's word. Josiah was troubled when his scribe showed him the scroll because he knew that the people of Judah had not followed God's wishes. He took the scroll to a prophet named Huldah, and she spoke for God, saying, "The people have not followed my wishes. They have worshipped other gods and forgotten my commandments about taking care of the poor. But because Josiah's heart was broken when he realized this, I will not destroy Jerusalem. You are my people, and I know you can do better." (Retold from 2 Kings 22)

What do you think the Bible is?
Who do you think wrote the Bible?
Why do you think the Bible is important?

The Bible is a book. Actually, it is many books written in different styles and languages that were put together into one book to tell the story of people throughout time and place trying to follow God. These books were written thousands of years ago, in places all around the

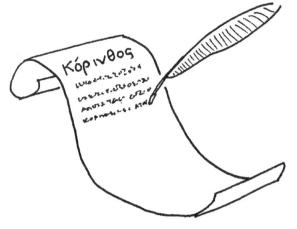

Middle East. Some tell the history of God's people. Some are poetry or songs that are written down. Some books are letters helping groups of people learn how to follow Jesus. The books about Jesus and his life and ministry are called gospels, which means "good news"! Throughout all the books that make up the Bible, God's love for us shines through.

We said what the Bible is. But we also need to say what the Bible is not. The Bible is not a rule book. It does not have the power to decide who is good and bad or worthy and unworthy of love. The Bible is not a book of science or a history book without opinions. The Bible is a collection of stories about God wanting to be in relationship with God's people. Humans wrote the books, and since humans are not perfect, they did not write everything there is to know about God. But as Christ followers, we believe that God speaks to us through the words in the Bible. When we study the Bible, we use our brains to be curious about the stories, and we use our hearts to guide us to God's words of love.

Who wrote the books? Well, lots of people did! We don't know all their names, but how and when and what they wrote gives us some clues to who they were. Mostly men, but maybe some women, wrote the books that eventually became the Bible.

Spiritual Practice: **Have you ever wondered who wrote a certain book in the Bible? Look at Philippians 1:1, Leviticus 1:1, and Isaiah 1:1. Can you find any clues about who wrote these books? Philippians tells us that it was written by Paul and Timothy. Leviticus doesn't say who the writer is. Isaiah is about one person's vision from God, but most people who study the Bible think this vision was written down by more than one person.**

How did the Bible come together? In the third and fourth centuries of the Common Era, some religious leaders had meetings to decide what books should go into the Bible. Humans decided what to include and what to leave out based on what that group of people thought was important to say about God. Today we know that some of the books and writings that got left out also have important things to tell us about God. The people who were in those meetings also decided the order of the books of the Bible. Today, most Christians use the same order of books, but some denominations, like Catholic and Episcopal churches, have extra books, called the Apocrypha. The Apocrypha is the section of the Bible containing books that the long-ago religious leaders decided were not inspired by God, but were still important to study and learn from.

What parts of the Bible do you like best? What parts of the Bible do you find confusing or troubling? What parts do you want to learn more about?

The Bible is important to more people than just Christians. The first part of the Bible is made up of the oldest books, written thousands of years ago and sacred to the Jewish tradition. Judaism calls these books the TaNaKh. The TaNaKh stands for the Hebrew names of each kind of book included: the Torah (Teachings), the Nevi'im (the Prophets), and the Ketuvim (the writings). Because Jesus was Jewish, the TaNaKh is the sacred text Jesus and his followers would have been familiar with.

Some Christians call the TaNaKh the Old Testament. Others call it the Hebrew Bible, because the TaNaKh contains the books that were sacred to the Hebrew people and they were originally written in the Hebrew language. Jewish people today still learn from the TaNaKh, even though Jewish practice has changed significantly over time. They also learn from the Talmud, a book that records many rabbis' conversations about the Hebrew Bible and the tradition that birthed what we know today as Judaism. The Talmud shows people that there are lots of ways to read sacred writings and that sometimes the interpretations change over time.

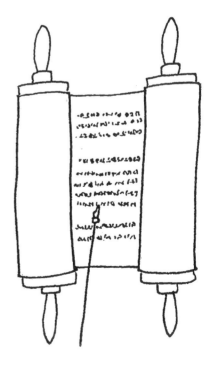

The second part of the Bible is called the New Testament. The New Testament is a collection of gospels, books that tell the stories of Jesus's life and ministry, and letters, sometimes called epistles, written by people who followed the Way of Jesus after Jesus's lifetime. The letters are usually addressed to a specific community, such as the Romans, the Philippians, and the Ephesians. The teachings and advice in the letters specifically address concerns that those communities were facing. All the New Testament books were written between 20 and 100 years after Jesus's life, as Jesus's followers tried to figure out who they were and how they were different from other ways of following the Jewish faith.

The Bible is special to lots of people around the world. Many religious traditions respect the Old Testament and the New Testament as containing wisdom for everyday living that encourages people to act justly to the world around them. Even though the Bible is a special book, the Bible is not God. God is so much bigger than humans can understand, so all of God's words can't be included in just one book. God is so vast that God cannot be contained in all the books humans could ever write.

Spiritual Practice: **Take some chalk outside to your driveway or a sidewalk near your home. Think about a simple message about God you want to share with people around you. Use words and pictures to express your message with the chalk. Have an adult take a photo of your message and send it to someone. By sharing a message with your community about your experience of God, you are doing what the biblical writers were doing. They were sharing an experience of God with their community. Maybe you, like the biblical writers, will inspire others to share their messages about God, too!**

Different groups of people have different ways of understanding the meaning of the Bible. Some think that if something is in the Bible, that means God said it and it's okay. But that way of reading doesn't honor the

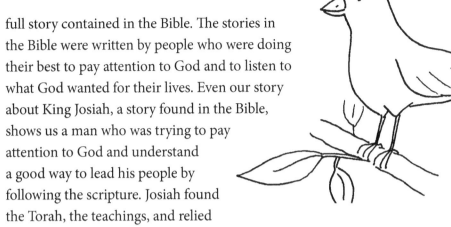

full story contained in the Bible. The stories in the Bible were written by people who were doing their best to pay attention to God and to listen to what God wanted for their lives. Even our story about King Josiah, a story found in the Bible, shows us a man who was trying to pay attention to God and understand a good way to lead his people by following the scripture. Josiah found the Torah, the teachings, and relied on it for guidance. Then his story also became a part of the Bible!

Because they are human, the authors and collectors of scriptures made mistakes. Some people use the Bible to find ways to divide people, looking for rules that place some people in power and push other people down. Reading the Bible in this way can have dangerous, even deadly, consequences, as people ignore the truth that all people are beloved. Sometimes people will look at one single verse from the Bible and not pay attention to what words are around it. That can be inspiring for some, but it rarely honors the expansiveness of God's messages to us about how we should live and behave.

Justice Story ~ *In the 1970s, when Nicaragua was under the rule of the Somoza dictatorship, a young Catholic priest and poet began a series of conversations about the Bible with campesinos in the Solentiname Archipelago in Lake Nicaragua. Father Ernesto Cardenal hosted conversations with up to 20 people at a time, inviting them to engage the Bible with their own life experiences, questions, and faith. The campesinos focused on themes of Jesus's care for the poor and resistance to powerful people dominating less powerful people. As they read, they dreamed of a kingdom of God in which people would have what they needed to not only survive but thrive. As they read and discussed the Bible in community, they wondered about the intention of the people who wrote down the stories about Jesus's life, and they even shared frustrations and confusion about the Bible. Together, the community that read the Bible together were able to gain deeper understandings of these sacred writings than if they interpreted it on their own. The Gospel in Solentiname is the collection of these conversations and is a resource for studying the Bible "from below" to Christians all over the world today.* ∼

Who reads the Bible with you? Who would you like to talk with about what you read in the Bible?

The Bible is just one way that humans encounter God. The words and stories and poems and teachings in this special book can help us learn about ourselves, our communities, and the world. The words of the Bible, though they don't change (except for with different translations), might seem to contain different messages for us depending on what is going on in our lives when we read them. In this way, the Bible contains "living words": words and stories that inspire us, challenge us, prompt us to think deeply, help us behave with kindness, and teach us about the complexity of the God we love and worship.

Spiritual Practice: **Choose a story from the Bible to read this week.**
Each day, read the story aloud several times, thinking about these questions after each reading:

> **What word or phrase calls to you?**
> **What do you wonder about this word or phrase?**
> **What do you think God is telling you through this word or phrase?**
> **What do you feel called to do in this word or phrase?**

Each day, read the same Bible story and ask the same questions.
At the end of the week, think about what you've learned about this story.
Did the story feel the same each day? Did you learn something different about the story by reading it on different days?

For younger children

SAY: The Bible has lots of stories, poems, histories, letters, and prayers all combined into one book. The Bible shares how people who lived long ago understood God. Part of it shares stories of God's people and God's special child, Jesus. We read the Bible to learn, pray, and wonder about God.

DO: Read some stories from the Bible. Which one is the most interesting?

PRAY: Dear God, thank you for the Bible and for all the ways that you speak to your people. Help me listen for your voice. Amen.

7
What Is Worship?

After God led the people of Israel out of slavery, they remembered how to be free people. They lived and worked without fear of oppression, and with God's vision leading them, made a new life together as they journeyed toward the Promised Land. They were also able to worship God without worry of what the Egyptians might say or do, and God gave them new instructions and ideas about how to worship. God offered them instructions on how they should gather and what sort of worship space to create. There were instructions for building and decorating the worship space, called the Tabernacle, and for how to pray. Worshipping God was the most important part of their life together, and the people gave their worship a lot of care, time, and concern for the smallest details. They wanted the ways that they prayed, sang, made offerings to God, treated one another, and made decisions for their community to be one beautiful and interconnected way of worshipping God. (Retold from Exodus 25)

The word "worship" means to express love, admiration, and respect. You might have heard this word used to describe what people do at church, like "worship service" or "Sunday worship," the time when Christians gather to sing, pray, read the Bible, hear a sermon, or share in rituals like communion.

Spiritual Practice: **How does your community or church worship together? What are some of your favorite parts of worshipping with your church?**

Take a few minutes to sing a song or pray a prayer that you know from your church worship right now. You can sing those songs and pray those prayers any time you like.

Different churches and denominations have their own special ways of worshipping God together. If you visit a new church, you might notice differences in the prayers, songs, space, and order from what you are used to. These changes might be big or small or might seem strange or exciting, but the differences show us all the beautiful ways that people express their love to God.

In the book of Exodus, God gave the people detailed instructions for how to worship. This part of the Bible includes ideas about how to create a space for worship, how to decorate it, how to say prayers, and how to choose leaders who would work to make all these things happen. Some Jewish and Christian communities still use the ideas from these ancient writings, but others do not. Over time, congregations have adjusted how they worship to meet people's needs while keeping a connection to the ancient ways.

When we read all these instructions about worship, the details are an invitation for us to be thoughtful and thorough in how we love God, to celebrate beauty, and to commit to gathering with other faithful people in worship. Much more than the songs we sing, candles we light, or spaces where we gather, worship is all about loving God and expressing that love. What are some other ways that you worship, or show your love for God, beyond worshipping at church?

We love and worship God when we think about God, read about God, and ask these big God questions.

You're worshipping God right now as you read this book, wonder, and learn!

We worship God when we say a blessing before a meal that offers thanks to God, the earth, and the workers who made eating the food possible.

Spiritual Practice: Do you ever say a blessing before you eat? Try this one out before your next meal or snack:

> **God is great.**
> **God is good.**
> **Let us thank God for our food.**
> **By God's hands we all are fed.**
> **Thank you, God, for our daily bread.**

Or you can sing this blessing (to the tune of "Frère Jacques") before a meal or at any time of day:

> **God our Father, God our Mother,**
> **Once again, once again,**
> **Thank you for our blessings,**
> **For our many blessings.**
> **Amen, amen.**

We worship God when we see a beautiful flower or the ocean and think, "Wow!"

Spiritual Practice: **Find time to take a walk outside. Whether you live in the busiest city or in the country or somewhere in between, look for, listen to, smell, and sense nature as you walk. Do you see plants or animals? Feel a cool breeze on your skin? Smell cut grass or fall leaves? Say aloud or silently to yourself, "Wow, God!" to honor everything that is around you!**

We worship God whenever we say "Thank you" or have an attitude of gratitude about things in our lives and the world.

Spiritual Practice: **Play a game of "I Spy" with a friend or alone, challenging yourself and each other to notice details in or around your home. After each thing you spy, take a big deep breath to pay extra attention, or say aloud, "Thank you, God, for _____."**

When we turn our attention and give love and thanks to God each day, it changes how we see the world around us and the things happening in our lives. We notice that life is full of gifts and beauty, even in the hardest times. We get better at remembering that God is with us always.

Justice Story ~ *When the coronavirus pandemic spread across the world, there were many things people didn't understand about how to keep each other safe. Scientists quickly learned that big indoor gatherings of people were spreading the virus. Leaders across the world urged people to listen to the scientists, making laws directing people not to gather in large groups and telling people to wear masks over their noses and mouths to protect each other. This meant that churches needed to change how they gathered, how they cared for their members and their communities, and how they worshipped God. Some churches used digital technology to record videos of music, prayers, and sermons to send to people in the congregation. Others used conference video and phone calls to gather people together for*

worship. Many churches used email and letters to share sermons, prayers, and words of encouragement with people. Some began to gather outdoors in parks and parking lots, spread far apart and wearing masks, to worship God together. Like many schools and businesses, churches had to change very quickly to be healthy and safe.

During this difficult, scary, and confusing time, the ways people worshipped God looked very different than before the pandemic and sometimes looked, sounded, and felt strange. It did not feel the same at all! People felt sad, confused, frustrated, worried, anxious, lonely, and so many more feelings. These changes also meant that people could worship in churches that were far away, reconnecting with a community they had moved away from or joining with family in other parts of the country or the world. They could even worship in a new way, trying dinner church or visiting a community of another faith. Because part of how we worship God is by committing to love everyone and keep each other safe and well, these changes in worship showed our commitment to God and our care for one another. ~

Have you ever worshipped God in a hard time? What happened?

We can worship God in so many ways and in so many different times in our lives. We can also worship God anywhere! We worship at church, when we're at the dinner table, and when we're out for a walk. It can be fun to set up a special place for worshipping at home, too.

Spiritual Practice: **Find a space in your home that can be your worship place. It might be a room, a closet, a corner, or even just one shelf. It might be a blanket that you can put out or fold away. You can choose items that help you focus on God to have in your worship space: a battery-powered candle to remind you of God's light; a nature treasure to remind you of God's beautiful creation; a Bible that you can read and remember the ways that God has loved us and the things Jesus taught us. This can be a spot for praying, reading Bible stories (or this book), singing songs about God, or taking deep breaths.**

For younger children

SAY: "Worship" means showing God our love. We worship when we learn about God, when we tell God "Thank you," and when we admire beauty and goodness around us.

DO: Learn and practice a meal blessing.

PRAY: Thank you! Wow! Amen.

8
What Is Prayer?

While Jesus was teaching his followers, he showed them how to pray. Jesus said, "When you worship God, don't do it to show off. Don't attract attention when you give to those in need. Only God knows your heart, so you don't need to impress others. When you pray, don't be like people who want to be seen being righteous. Instead, pray when you are alone, when only God can hear you. And when you pray, be careful with your words so that you mean them. God knows what we need before we ask, so be honest with God and open your heart in prayer. Use words like this:

"Our Creator, who is in heaven,
Your name is precious to us and we honor it.
Bring your kingdom to us on earth, so that our relationships will honor
    heaven.
Give us what we need for today.
Forgive us for the ways we have wronged you by wronging others,
And help us forgive those who have wronged us.
Lead us away from temptation, and deliver us from those who would
    do evil." (Retold from Matthew 6 and Luke 11)

Prayer is communication with God. It is what we do when we feel like we need to talk to God. But it is also a lot more than that! Prayer is being close with God and paying attention to God. We can pray with or without words. We are in prayer when we notice what God is doing around us in the world, each and every day.

What do you notice God doing each day? How do you communicate with God?

Jesus taught his disciples a simple way to pray. Part of the prayer Jesus taught, which we call the Lord's Prayer, is proclaiming who God is. We say what we know about God to respect God: we know that God is our creator who gives us life; that God is in some ways separate from the world; and that God's name is precious and we know it is right to honor God's name. When we describe God's character, we are honoring the Sacred by showing that we know who we are and who God is.

The other part of the prayer is about human needs: peace and justice like in God's kingdom; daily needs like food and safety; forgiveness to heal our relationships with humans and with God; and resistance to temptations to sin and hurt our relationships. Jesus taught his followers to ask, like the Israelites in the wilderness did (Exodus 16:4), only for what they needed that one day, so that people wouldn't hoard what they had but be content with simple needs. Humans also can pray for God to help heal relationships by forgiving and resisting temptation.

The Lord's Prayer (in Matthew 6 and Luke 11) is not the only prayer in the Bible. The poems or songs in the book of Psalms are very old prayers. We don't know who wrote the Psalms, though many people think King David wrote some of them. The Psalms show us that human prayers remain the same, though people change across time and space. Prayer expresses however we are feeling to God. God can handle all our feelings: gratitude and joy, blessing and request, asking for help and crying out in sadness and pain and anger. Sometimes we have "sighs too deep for words" and sometimes our prayers don't make a lot of sense.

When and where do you see, hear, or pray the Lord's Prayer?
What other prayers do you know? How did you learn those prayers?

We pray with our bodies. When our bodies are in comfortable positions, we can focus on how our breath and our heartbeat help us live. This reminds us how God breathed life into us in the beginning of creation and how our heartbeat reminds us of Jesus our brother. Some people pray with their hands folded together, and some people pray on their knees. Some people turn their faces toward the ground to acknowledge how the earth holds us up and to respect God. Others turn their face toward the sky to remember how God is all around us.

Prayer can be quiet, like if you pray with words in your mind or whisper softly or think about God without speaking. Prayer can also be loud, as it might be if you are crying or if you are singing or if you have big feelings and need to express them with loud noise. Prayer can be still if you sit or lie down and focus on keeping your body in one place. Prayer can be full of movement if you feel close to God when you dance or run or play sports or rock a baby. You might feel like praying when you spend time in nature, when you hike in the woods or play in the sand or swim in the ocean. You can listen to or make music as a prayer. You can help someone plant a garden or share a meal as a prayer. You can draw and paint and knit and color and sculpt and collage as a prayer. Every single person prays differently. You can try different kinds of prayer to find what helps you connect with God.

Spiritual Practice: How do you pray? Find a space with few distractions where you can move comfortably. Choose a simple phrase, like "God be with me" or "I rest in God" or "Give us your peace." Repeat in your mind as you do each of these poses.

By moving our bodies intentionally, we honor God's gift of life. Yoga is a Hindu prayer practice. Today, people of many different faith traditions and no faith practice yoga for health and meditation. Stand or sit up as straight as you can, with your arms at your side and your palms facing forward (mountain pose). Take a deep breath in this position. Then slowly move your hands above your head with your palms facing inward. Take a deep breath in this position.

Next, sit on the floor with your legs crisscross-applesauce (easy pose). Sit up as straight as you can and take a few big breaths. Try to lengthen your spine by imagining a string pulling your head straight up to the sky.

Next, lie down with your arms at your side (corpse pose) and breathe deeply. To finish, bring your knees to your chest and grab your feet (happy baby pose). Breathe deeply. You can even roll around on the ground in happy baby pose.

You can pray anywhere. At home, before meals, at school, at church, on the playground. You can pray when you're alone, before you go to bed or when you're doing your homework or when you're on the bus. Or you can pray with your friends or family or church. You can pray for any reason. You can pray when you don't know what else to do, or you can pray because you love to talk to God.

Sometimes praying in groups, like in church during worship or before a community meal, can be helpful for processing big feelings. When one person is struggling or having an intense emotion, praying with others can help uplift that person and help them remember they are not alone. Or when someone is happy or rejoicing, praying with others shares the joy. When churches pray together, sometimes they will confess how they've made mistakes or done something harmful and ask forgiveness. The whole community can then help each other forgive and do better. Other times the church will ask God to help them live, ask God to lead them in bringing justice and creating peace in the world. When the whole group prays together, they witness each other and promise to help each other.

When do you pray? Where do you pray?
Do you pray alone or with other people?
What is your favorite way to pray?

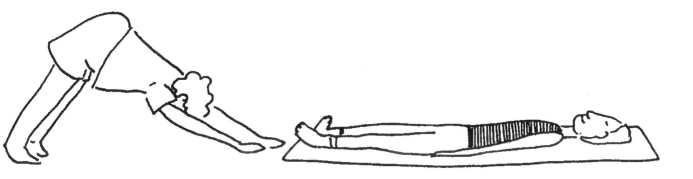

Justice Story ~ **In 1965, Rabbi Abraham Joshua Heschel joined Dr. Martin Luther King Jr. and other interfaith clergy and movement activists on the Selma-to-Montgomery march during the Civil Rights Movement. After the march, someone asked Rabbi Heschel if he had found time to pray during the march and demonstrations. Rabbi Heschel said he prayed with his feet. Today, faith leaders of many traditions, both ordained and laypeople, accompany activists in social justice movements as "movement chaplains." They embrace the words of Rabbi Heschel and understand that protesting, marching, and participating in direct action for social justice are also prayers. The God who cares especially for the oppressed and the outcast empowers some people to pray by supporting social movements and witnessing what God is doing among activists and peacemakers.** ~

When we pray, it is natural to want to ask God for things. Maybe it's to help heal a relationship. Maybe we ask God for forgiveness for when we said something rude or did something unkind. Perhaps we pray to feel God's presence, or for peace, or for comfort when we are hurting. When we ask God for something, we need to know that God doesn't always answer our prayers in the way we expect. Sometimes we don't even realize that God has answered our prayers because we are looking for something different than God is giving us. Just because we don't get what we ask for doesn't mean that God isn't listening or isn't real. We can't pray more or harder to make God change a situation. Sometimes we will think about a situation that we prayed about a long time ago and realize that we did receive an answer to our prayer, but we didn't know it at the time. Whatever we pray for and however we pray, God always listens to our prayers, always reaches out toward the Creation to listen to our pains and joys and questions and thanksgivings.

What have you prayed about in the past? What happened?

In Romans 8, the apostle Paul wrote that the Holy Spirit prays in us. When we pray, we are making room for God in our lives. Sometimes prayer is easy and comforting, and sometimes it can feel more like wrestling. God can handle all our emotions and every situation that we pray about. God's presence is always with us, whether we feel it at the time or not.

Spiritual Practice: Think about something you want to tell God. Maybe you want to ask for help with something. Maybe you want to give thanks to God. Keep your prayer simple so you can say it over a few times. The first time, say it in your regular speaking voice. The second time, say it loudly or shout it. The third time, whisper your prayer quietly. Notice how it feels to pray at different volumes. What kinds of prayers need to be shouted? What kinds of prayers need to be whispered? However you need to pray about what is in your heart, God is with you and listening to you.

For younger children

SAY: Prayer is talking to God, being close to God, and paying attention to God all around us. We can pray by talking to God, taking deep breaths, singing, or making something. We can pray to God about anything, anywhere, anytime.

DO: Try a body prayer pose.

PRAY: Ask children, "What would you like to tell God today?"

9
Where Is God When Bad Things Happen?

Once upon a time there was a man named Job, who was kind and loving, who worked hard and cared for his community and family. Terrible things began to happen to him, things that no one should ever experience. Storms with lightning burned up his farm. Bad guys took his farm animals. Job's friends, workers, and children were hurt and even died in terrible accidents. Job became very sick: he had sores on his skin, and his body hurt all over. He asked God for help in prayer. When other people tried to understand why these bad things had happened, they told him terrible, hurtful ideas. Job's friends told him that he must have done something wrong to deserve all these bad things.

Finally, Job and God had a conversation, and God explained a strange answer for why bad things happen: there is not always a good answer. Job asked God to explain where God had been and why God hadn't protected him. But instead of talking about the hard things Job experienced, God told him all about the strange creatures, the beautiful earth, the powerful sea that God created. God talked about God's wisdom, about everything strange and beautiful that is beyond human beings' ability to know. Job remembered that some hard questions don't have a clear answer, but no matter what happens he could trust that God was there. (Retold from the Book of Job)

Spiritual Practice: **Sometimes we have hard days, and sometimes terrible things happen in our lives. Has anything hard or terrible ever happened to** you? What happened? Put one hand on your belly and one hand on your heart. Take three big deep breaths. After you breathe in, say, "I am right here." After you breathe out, say, "I am right now."

Sometimes it is easy to talk about hard or scary times. Sometimes it is hard to talk about them. Everyone, at some point in their lives, feels frightened or hurt or lonely.

Spiritual Practice: **If it's not easy for you to talk or think about your hard time today, you might like to take some time to make art. The art doesn't have to be a picture of the hard time. Sometimes creating pictures, shapes, or colors is just very good for our mind, feelings, and bodies, especially when we have been through something tough.**

The story about Job in the Bible is strange and simple at the same time. It is an unusual kind of story in the Bible, because it is a sort of myth or legend that people would tell to explain where God is when bad things happen.

It seems surprising that all these bad things happened to someone at the same time, but we might know the feeling of when bad things just keep adding up. When we read about Job's friends, it might seem obvious that they were saying some really unhelpful things, but we have probably had the feeling of someone trying to be kind and actually saying something unkind. We may have even been the person who accidentally said a hurtful thing!

What would you like someone to say or do for you if you were going through a hard time or feeling sad?

Even when we are being well cared for, when people show and speak love to us, hard and painful things are still hard and painful! We might wonder: Why is this happening to me? What is the point of this? Will things be okay again someday? Maybe like Job, who experienced some very hard times, we find ourselves wondering: Where is God? Can God fix this bad thing?

One of the most important things that we know about God and hard things is this: God never makes bad things happen to us or to anyone else. Hard and hurting times are not a test or punishment, no matter what. The Bible says that "every good gift, every perfect gift, comes from above. These gifts come down from the Father, the creator of the heavenly lights, in whose character there is no change at all" (James 1:17, Common English Bible). God is the cause and giver of good things, not bad. We can trust God's character, God's personality—and, most important, God's values—to be consistent with goodness, not badness.

Some bad things happen because of the patterns of nature. Things like earthquakes, fierce animals hurting people, even sickness can be hard and terrible, but we are part of a larger natural world in which the earth and other creatures are also trying to live and flourish. Those land shifts, animals in self-protection, and microbes can cause humans harm just by doing what they are supposed to do.

Some bad things happen because people make mistakes. Breaking a bone while playing outside, car crashes, missing a party or an important appointment—all happen and for no reason other than no one's body or mind is perfect. We aren't superheroes, and people make mistakes.

Some bad things happen because people make terrible choices. War, the ways that the earth and climate are changing and hurting, and people not having a safe place to live or enough food to eat—all happen because human beings choose their own power and comfort over the well-being of all persons and the natural world.

In all these different kinds of bad things, it is okay to be angry and sad. It is okay to be scared. It is fantastic if you think about these bad things and decide you want to get to work at changing them!

A very important thing for us to know and remember is that God is always with us, even in hard times. The apostle Paul, who experienced many difficult times in his life, wrote:

I'm convinced that nothing can separate us from God's love in Christ Jesus our Lord, not death or life, not angels nor rulers, not present things or future things, not powers or height or depth, or any other thing that is created. (Romans 8:38, Common English Bible)

No matter what happens, God's love is always with us.

Spiritual Practice: **Fill in the blanks with your own examples. "Nothing can separate me from God's love. Not _____ or _____ or _____."**

One way that we remember that God's love is with us is by experiencing love and care from our communities during a hard time. Not everyone says silly things like Job's friends! In fact, most of the time people are very loving and helpful.

Justice Story — *In 2017 a very strong storm, Hurricane Harvey, came to Texas, and many people in Houston lost their homes or had to leave them for a time until the winds stopped blowing and the flood waters went down. It is a frightening thing to experience a hurricane. One man, Jim McIngvale, wanted to help his friends and neighbors. Jim owned a store that sold furniture, called Gallery Furniture. He used his furniture delivery trucks to give people a ride to safety. If people needed a safe place to stay and rest, he hosted them at the furniture store, where there were plenty of comfortable couches and chairs and cozy beds. Jim saw a need in his community, as people were having a very hard time, and thought about how he might have something to help. He showed loving presence in a practical way to so many neighbors and community members. God's love for Houston was shown through Jim's love. God was in Jim.*

When we remember stories like this, stories of people helping, caring, and working together to support those in need or harm, we can see God's love everywhere, even in the toughest and saddest times.

Whose love and care remind you that God's love is here? To whom do you show God's love?

God's Spirit and love are always with you, no matter what happens in your life or in the world. You can find God's presence in loving and kind people around you. You can find God when you pray or take deep, calming breaths. You can find God when you read or listen to stories of how God always takes care of people and how people take care of each other.

Spiritual Practice: **After you finish reading this chapter, find someone you love and trust and give them a big hug or a hand squeeze to remind yourself and them that we are not alone.**

For younger children

SAY: God is with us, no matter what. When bad things happen, we feel God's love through other people showing love and kindness to us.

DO: Ask, "When have you had a hard time? What happened?"

PRAY: God, thank you for loving me when things are hard or scary. Thank you for never leaving me. Amen.

10
Why Did Jesus Die?

When it was nearly time for the Passover festival, Jesus and his disciples travelled to Jerusalem. When they arrived in Jerusalem, crowds of people welcomed him because they had heard of his ministry. Some of the religious leaders and government officials didn't like Jesus. They worried he would turn the people against them. They planned a way to arrest Jesus.

After eating a meal together, Jesus and his friends went to a garden to pray. While Jesus was praying, a crowd came and arrested Jesus. The soldiers crucified Jesus. People walking by insulted Jesus and the criminals who were killed near him. The women who had travelled with Jesus watched from a distance, including Jesus's mother, Mary. Then, Jesus died.

Later that day, a man who had followed Jesus, named Joseph, asked for Jesus's body, so that he could be buried with respect. Joseph took Jesus's body down from the cross. Joseph wrapped the body gently in clean cloths, and laid it in a tomb that was carved in rock. He closed the tomb by rolling a stone in front of the entrance. The women who had been there the whole time kept watch over the place where Jesus's body lay. (Retold from Matthew 26–27)

Jesus was born in a part of the Roman Empire called Judea, where Herod was the king. Jesus grew up in the Jewish tradition. Usually, Jewish people didn't have to worship Roman gods, because they didn't cause a lot of trouble and the government didn't think they threatened the stability of the empire. But sometimes leaders would come forward and say that the people should not have to follow the Roman emperor's laws because they should follow God's laws instead. These people were called prophets. They spoke God's truth about justice to people in power. Jesus was a leader like this.

Herod, the king of Judea, worried about other leaders being more popular than him. When Jesus was born, Herod heard that people were talking about a child born who was called "King of the Jews." Herod was so jealous of a baby having this title that he ordered his soldiers to find all young boys who were the same age as this child. Jesus's parents were warned that Herod wanted to harm Jesus, and they knew the powerful king would bully and threaten until he got his way, so they travelled to Egypt until the threat was gone.

As Jesus grew up and began his ministry and people began to follow him, again Herod became anxious. He worried that if people listened to Jesus, who was preaching about love and justice, they would follow Jesus. He worried that if Jesus kept healing people and feeding people, the people would like Jesus more than Herod. Maybe the people would even overthrow Herod and his family, ending their powerful reign. If it was possible to overturn the government of the region of Judea, then maybe it was even possible to overturn the government of the whole Roman Empire.

How do the stories and teachings of Jesus make you feel?
Which Jesus stories feel hopeful to you?
Which Jesus stories feel scary or uncomfortable to you?

The Gospels, the books that tell the stories of Jesus's life, tell us that not everyone was a fan of

Jesus. Some people even feared and hated him. Some of these people were Herod and his family. Others were political and religious leaders who disagreed with Jesus. Others were Roman politicians who did not like that Jesus was talking about the kingdom of God being more powerful than Rome. All these people watched Jesus closely.

Jesus knew that he was being watched and that his followers were threatened. His cousin, John the Baptist, was killed for prophesying that a leader like Jesus was on his way. Jesus knew that doing what was right was dangerous. Jesus kept on going, helping the poor and the oppressed and healing the sick and feeding the hungry. He gave instructions to his disciples about what to do if something bad happened to him (John 16).

How do you think these people stayed brave as they followed Jesus? What makes you feel brave?

Eventually, Jesus was arrested. He was given a trial in front of powerful people who did not approve of what he was teaching and preaching. Then Jesus was brought before Pontius Pilate, the Roman governor. He ordered Jesus to be killed. The Roman soldiers bullied Jesus and hurt his body. Then, they nailed him to a cross.

People mocked Jesus while his body hung on the cross. They had heard the people calling Jesus the Messiah. They thought the Messiah was supposed to be a powerful warrior. People said, "If he is the chosen one of God, why doesn't he save himself?" The people watching Jesus die didn't know what to think.

Jesus died on the cross. He had done his best to live according to God's way of love. He preached justice. He healed people. He welcomed strangers and outcasts. People remembered how he lived for a long, long time. You are remembering right now, reading this book.

How can following God's way of love be dangerous? What kinds of risks do we have to take when we love people?

Jesus died because his ministry and preaching calling for justice for the oppressed threatened the way of life that kept powerful people in charge. Jesus himself was an outsider, a brown-skinned man from a small village

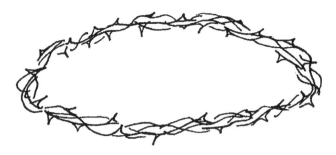

far from the city. The people who followed him were a threat, too, because they agreed with Jesus that the violence of the Roman Empire should not continue. Jesus and his followers knew that another world was possible, that all people could live with dignity if they were not being overshadowed by those in power. Because Jesus loved all people and was doing ministry to make their lives better, the powerful tried to end his work for justice.

What stories do you know about people who do the right thing, even when it is dangerous? Why were the people who followed Jesus also a threat?

God never left Jesus or turned away, even when Jesus was enduring the pain of the cross. This is a promise we know today, too: God will be with us always. In the Gospels, God shows us that death is never the end of the story. Jesus's resurrection is one example of this. Like a seed, Jesus was buried in the ground. It seemed like there was no life present. Then, on the third day after his death, Jesus rose to be alive again. Sometimes the things that die must decay and be buried, going back to the earth from which they grew. Jesus, like all of us, went back to the earth, and then he became alive again to remind us that death is not the answer. It is not the end. The powers and principalities, the empires of the world, cannot control love. They cannot stamp out justice, because the fires of justice burn continuously, and God is breathing new life into things that seem dead every day.

Spiritual Practice: **With a piece of paper to write or draw on, or in conversation with your grownups, reflect on your day. This reflection will follow the pattern of the Examen, a method Saint Ignatius of Loyola used to consider where he felt close to or far away from or challenged by God.**

To make this easier to picture, imagine a rosebush: there are roses, thorns, and buds. Each part is different and has its own purpose, but they are all parts of the same plant. There will always be joys, difficulties, and opportunities for growth in our lives. Invite each person to name a rose (a joyful or happy thing they've experienced), a thorn (a sad, challenging, or painful thing they've experienced), and a bud (something they are looking forward to, something that has potential). It is normal to feel like God is near and God is far away all at the same time. We can learn from each part of the rose without judgment.

Every day, people like you challenge the harmful teachings and behaviors of the powerful. To speak truth and to show up for justice takes courage, the kind of courage that Jesus had when challenging the people who were oppressing others. Sometimes it can feel like we are not good enough or smart enough or brave enough to make a difference in the world. Sometimes we think, "Who would ever listen to me?" or "I'm just one person, what change can I make?" But you are not the only person thinking those thoughts and feeling those feelings. When people work together and unite around a shared goal, they change the world. Jesus was one person, but the movement that followed him continued his work even after he was gone.

Justice Story ~ **The Highlander Center in the foothills of the Appalachian Mountains in eastern Tennessee has been a sacred place to many activists, artists, organizers, and peacemakers for nearly 100 years. Founded by justice-minded people who opposed racial segregation, the Highlander Center was an important location for nonviolent civil disobedience trainings that were utilized in the Civil Rights Movement and many other movements since. The center gathered union organizers, teachers, resistance trainers, and workers' rights activists over the years to equip and mobilize people dedicated to justice for the oppressed. Because of these activities, the center has been the target of violence, sometimes receiving threats via letter and phone call, and people have even broken and burned their buildings. Though the archives,** *containing writings and speeches and memorabilia from Civil Rights leaders like Rev. Dr. Martin Luther King Jr. and Stokely Carmichael, was burned to the ground, the story of justice lived out there remains strong. The work of peacemaking could not be kept down, and the Highlander Center and all who have learned from their good work press on. People making change in many parts of the world began in this small outpost at the foot of the mountains, singing and praying and learning and organizing to build a better world where all are free.* ~

You don't need to be a superhero or the president or a famous person to make the world a more loving, generous, and just place. You just need to be you, knowing the truth that God loves all people. You can show this truth by encouraging your neighbors to treat each other with justice. Sometimes the smallest, simplest acts of love show people that another world is possible . . . and they make that other world happen.

For younger children

SAY: Jesus healed people and taught that God's love was for everyone, and many people were following him. This made the king and other leaders afraid that he would try to be in charge. They thought that when Jesus died, people would stop following him. Instead, God gave Jesus new life to show everyone God's love is stronger than anything, even death.

DO: Try a short form of the Examen at the end of the day: When were you joyful? Sad? Hopeful?

PRAY: Dear God, thank you for always being with Jesus, even in the scariest time. Thank you for always being with me, too. Amen.

11

What Is Resurrection?

After Jesus was killed, his friends took his body and put it in a grave called a tomb, a small room cut out of rock. They wrapped his body in cloth and closed the big stone door. The Roman governor had soldiers guarding the tomb because Jesus had been so dynamic in his teaching and healing and many people had been following him. On the third day after he died, women who were his friends went to the tomb to grieve for their friend. When they got to the place he had been buried, there was a big earthquake as an angel came and moved away the tomb's stone door. The Roman guards were so surprised and frightened that they fainted! The angel looked at Jesus's friends and said, "Don't be afraid. Jesus is not here anymore. He was raised from the dead, just like he said! Go and tell your other friends this good news!" (Retold from Matthew 28)

When we read the story of Jesus's crucifixion, how he was killed by the Roman empire because of his revolutionary life and call for earth-changing love, our hearts break and our spirits sink. But when we read on, we find that the story is not over!

The Gospels tell us that when the women who were Jesus's friends and family went to visit the place he was buried, there was no body. Jesus was gone! Was he missing? No. Stolen? No. Hidden? No, he was alive again! The big stone door of his burial place had been moved away, and Jesus was walking and talking, heart beating, loving, alive again!

After his friends learned the remarkable, frightening, joyful news that Jesus was alive, Jesus visited them and spent time with the people he loved. He showed them the places on his body where he had been hurt before his death and offered them encouragement and comfort after the sad and hard week they had experienced. He cooked a beach picnic for his friends and served them fish for breakfast. He told stories and taught. He went on walks with his friends. You can read all these stories in Matthew 28, Mark 16, Luke 24, and John 20–21.

Spiritual Practice: **Pick two of these stories in the Bible to read. How are the stories of resurrection different? How are they alike? Make a list of what you notice between the stories.**

Each of the Gospels, the four books of the Bible that tell the stories of Jesus, has a slightly different story about this event. The Bible is a beautiful and complicated book, and these four perspectives about one thing are an amazing example of how the Bible works. We see four different ways that people experienced an amazing encounter with God's presence in Jesus, and they all noticed different things. These different perspectives and ideas of Jesus and the resurrection are a great gift to us because they remind us that variety is beautiful and important for how we think about God!

Christianity calls these stories the "resurrection," a word that means "arise again." Some people have wondered if Jesus was just sleeping, and even thought that his friends had just stolen his dead body away and made up this story. Even his own dear friends and disciples that saw him were confused about what had happened! But Christianity across the years and in different traditions and cultures teaches that Jesus really did die on the cross, and Jesus really was alive again. He was not a ghost or a zombie; he was himself, alive! It is a strange mystery.

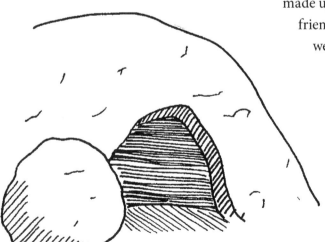

What do you think about this mystery? What do you imagine Jesus was like after the resurrection?

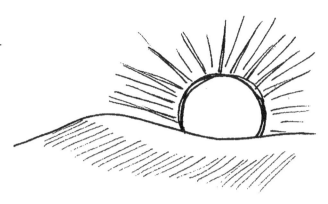

Every year the church celebrates and remembers this story on Easter Sunday. Some traditions call this Resurrection Sunday, and different forms of Christianity honor this celebration in different ways. There is usually a reading or retelling of one of the Gospel resurrection stories. Some communities sing, pray, share communion, have baptisms, or maybe even hunt for Easter eggs.

How do you celebrate Easter? Who celebrates with you?

We celebrate Easter again and again every year because we need a reminder of this important story of Jesus's life, but the importance of his resurrection isn't only important on Easter day. Any time we remember or have an experience of life and love winning out with persistence after even the hardest or meanest things, we are experiencing Easter.

When Jesus was resurrected, made alive, and raised again, he showed us that love and life are the most powerful things in the world. Jesus showed us that even when everything is awful and impossible, hope and love are still working all around. We see this power of life and love when flowers grow through sidewalk cracks. We see this power of life and love when we forgive each other. We see this power of life and love when people can go through impossibly hard and terrible things and still find joy, hope, and justice in the world.

Spiritual Practice: **What does life and love feel like? Close your eyes and take deep breaths. See if you can notice what life and love feel like in your body. Are there words to describe it? Are there movements that can express what life and love feel like to you?**

Justice Story ~ One story that shows the power of life and love to win in impossible situations is the story behind the Malala Fund, an international network that supports educating girls in communities where leaders think girls should not have access to learning and opportunity. The fund is named after Malala Yousafzai, a woman from Pakistan. Her father was a teacher at a girls' school and always believed in educating girls. But then unjust leaders took over their town and closed the school for girls. Malala, then just a young girl, and her father spoke out for girls' education and spoke out against the occupation of their community by harmful people. Malala wrote, spoke, and taught about how important educating girls and women is for all communities.

Not everyone was happy about her work; some people did not want things to change or girls to have an education. One day, while she was riding a bus, a man shot Malala! She was hurt very badly and spent a long time in the hospital. This attack was horrible and frightening, and many people had heard what happened to her and were shocked and angry. As Malala's body healed, she returned to her work of speaking out and making her

community better. Since more people knew about her and heard the message, one girl's story and the work of her community became a giant worldwide project. Despite and through something terrible and harmful, a beautiful and powerful force of love and life emerged.

Malala Yousafzai is not a Christian. Her cultural and religious heritage is Sunni Muslim, a religion that believes in Jesus in a different way than Christians do. However, she does not need to be a Christian for us to see that in her story and her community's story, life and love won out over harm and pain. The deepest, truest idea of resurrection that we understand in the story of Jesus shows up in many different people, places, and stories. ~

One of the ways that Jesus talked about his own death and resurrection with his friends was with the symbol of a seed or a kernel of wheat. He said, "unless a grain of wheat falls into the earth and dies, it remains just a single grain; but if it dies, it bears much fruit" (John 12:24). A seed that is not planted is just a useless little thing, but when it is buried, it rises again as a useful and beautiful plant. It can

even create many more seeds and plants! We are like seedlings from the Jesus plant, and we grow strong and sprout our beautiful love and life into the world because he did.

Spiritual Practice: **Try growing a seed into a plant. It doesn't have to be fancy; a bean is great! Any container of soil will work, and if you don't have a seed to plant, try planting a dried bean or a cutting from a potato. Remember to give the seed water and sunshine. Watch for a sprout and see what happens!**

For younger children

SAY: "Resurrection" means being brought back to life. After Jesus died, God brought him back to life. This story shows us that love and life are more powerful than any hate or hurting in the world. We can find powerful new love and life, resurrection, in many places in our lives and world.

DO: Plant a seed and watch it grow.

PRAY: Dear God, thank you for your power and life. Help me remember that love always wins. Amen.

12

What Is Baptism?

John the Baptist was a man who preached in the wild places of the land of Judea. John called people to remember their God. He said to them, "Turn your lives to focus on God, for the kingdom of the Holy is close to Creation." People came to John from all over, meeting him by the River Jordan and confessing the ways they'd done wrong to God and to their neighbors. Then John baptized them in the river. Jesus of Nazareth traveled to the Jordan River to be baptized by John. They went into the water of the river, and when Jesus came out of the water, the heavens were opened and the Holy Spirit, looking like a dove, came down to Jesus. Then all who were at the river heard the voice of the Holy saying, "This is my beloved child, whom I love." (Retold from Matthew 3)

All people are connected to water. Water is all around us: in lakes and rivers and oceans, in clouds and raindrops and snowflakes, and in plants, animals, and even you and me! Our bodies are made of water. Water that falls to the ground as rain goes into the soil, then runs into rivers and oceans. This happens over and over again as water is recycled. That means the water that is inside each tiny cell of our body is water that has been in rivers and streams, in clouds and polar ice, making plants and animals and other humans alive for thousands of years. Over time, humans learned how to store water and clean it and use it for cooking, washing, farming, and eventually turn it into electric power. Water is so important to life that almost every society has rituals honoring water's power and mystery.

What is your favorite way of using water?
What are important ways you use water?

Water is important in the Bible. Genesis 1 tells us that in the time before creation, waters covered the earth. In the Old Testament, God's people come through the waters to freedom. People meet each other at wells, relationships are mended at rivers, and the prophets say God's justice covers everything like a waterfall.

Water is important in Jesus's life, too. In the beginning of his ministry, Jesus is baptized in the Jordan River by John the Baptist. Later in his life, Jesus washes the disciples' feet with water and tells them to do the same for others. Water is important to Christians because it reminds us of Jesus's experiences with water: when we feel the water touch our bodies, it is a reminder of how Jesus went down into the water and then came up again. This is like how Jesus died and was buried, then was resurrected into new life.

Baptism is a ritual for welcoming a person into Christian community. It is a way for the gathered community to affirm someone's Christian identity and commit to helping that person grow in their faith. It is also a ritual that is special for the individual, marking a moment when they participated in recognizing God's grace in their lives and responding to that grace. When someone is baptized, they are turning away from sin, a word that means things that come between people and God, and they are turning toward Jesus, to follow him.

Sometimes people use words about cleanliness or purity when talking about baptism. For example, someone might say that baptism "washes away the dirt of sin" or "cleans us as white as snow." These words might seem simple, but they communicate that the whiter something, or someone, is, the better they are. Sadly, over time some humans with lighter skin tones have used these words to harm people who have darker shades of skin. We know that all skin colors are beautiful and worthy and beloved by God, so it is important for us to use different words to express the power of baptism.

What words could you use to talk about God's love and grace through baptism?

Each Christian denomination and even different churches have their own ways of doing baptism. Baptism can be a rite of passage that people look forward to because it is an important ritual in many churches, but it is not the end of a journey, a point of arrival. Baptism is a beginning.

Some communities celebrate baptism when people are babies or when someone joins the church. In other communities, baptism is practiced when people are old enough to choose to do the ritual. Some churches use a small cup or a shell to pour water over a person's head, and some churches have a baptismal font or pool that people can be fully immersed in. Some traditions even go to the nearest body of water, so people in their congregation are baptized in a river, lake, or ocean!

When and where have you seen a baptism? What happened during the baptism?

God is the giver of all good gifts. And humans have a choice for how we respond to those gifts, which we sometimes call "grace": we get to choose to follow in the Way of Jesus. Baptism is one way that people choose. For churches that practice "believer's baptism," the person being baptized makes a choice when they feel ready to publicly proclaim their faith and ask for help as they grow in their Christian journey. For churches that practice infant baptism, the adults who care for the baby make the choice to go through this ritual to show they will raise the child to know the Way of Jesus.

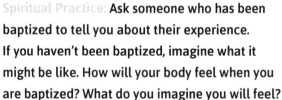 Spiritual Practice: **Ask someone who has been baptized to tell you about their experience. If you haven't been baptized, imagine what it might be like. How will your body feel when you are baptized? What do you imagine you will feel?**

No matter when in life a person is baptized, it is not something that one person can do alone. When Jesus was baptized, John the

Baptist was in the River Jordan with Jesus, and there were people standing on the banks watching and witnessing. Baptism is a ritual that happens in a community. The community of faith are witnesses who commit to pray for, help, and encourage the person being baptized in living their faith. When babies are baptized, the congregation promises the parents or guardians of the child that they will help raise the child in the faith and encourage the parents or guardians along the way. When older children or adults are baptized, they share how they will turn their lives toward God. The congregation listens to the person being baptized and promises to love and support that person as they grow in their faith.

Baptism is also a commitment to a community of faith, that the person being baptized will participate in the life of the congregation and use their God-given gifts to enrich the life of the community. When you become a part of a church community, you have a responsibility to care for others and to do your best to serve your church and help fulfill its mission. If you or someone you love is considering baptism, encourage them to talk to their pastor or another spiritual leader they trust.

Spiritual Practice: **Each time you wash your hands or drink a glass of water or swim in a lake or ocean, remember the waters of your baptism. Water is sacred and has memory. At the beginning of all things, Creation was covered with waters. At the beginning of human life, babies emerge from the waters of the womb. Baptism is in some ways a new beginning, a starting again, a renewing promise to remain connected to the Source of all Life, the Living Water.**

Justice Story ~ *God loves each and every person on this planet. It doesn't matter what religious tradition someone practices, or where someone lives, or what their race, ethnicity, nationality, gender, or sexuality are. God sees every person as their true selves, created to love and be loved.*

Some people are born with a body that doesn't match who they know they are in their heart. When people are born, usually a doctor will look at the baby and assign a biological sex to the baby based on the body parts the baby has. But as a person grows and becomes

more themselves, that person might realize the words and ideas their culture associates with the biological sex doesn't fit who they really are. These people might talk to their family, friends, church, and school and ask them to call them by a name that person chooses and use gender pronouns (like she, he, they, ze, etc.) that match their true self. Using the right name and pronouns for someone who is transgender or gender nonconforming shows that person that you love and respect them. Transgender people show us the diversity of God's good Creation.

Everyone deserves to live a healthy and whole life being who God created them to be in their heart. Sometimes transgender people will have a celebration or a ritual that marks the importance of living in the world as their authentic self. This might include a naming ceremony that marks their transition to living openly and being known by their chosen name. A naming ceremony is like a baptism because it is a special time when a community recognizes God's creation of a transgender person as their authentic self. This is also an opportunity for their community to welcome, affirm, celebrate, and commit to supporting the person in their faith journey.

When Clara, a teenager living in Texas, transitioned, it was important to her to mark this moment with a Renaming Liturgy ritual in her home church. Though it took a while for Clara to be ready to claim her true identity, God knew from the very beginning who Clara was. This ceremony gave her family, friends, and church community an opportunity to celebrate Clara living as her authentic self. Part of the liturgy reads, "This new name is the culmination of a journey of discovery and, at the same time, a new beginning."* As the church promised to love and support her, they used her correct name and pronouns. Clara's church reissued her baptism certificate

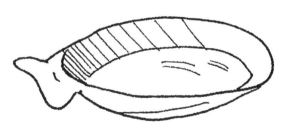

with her new name, honoring her baptism into the body of Christ as her true self.

God loves transgender people through their whole lives, and God rejoices when each person is loved and accepted and celebrated for who they are.

---

* "A Service of Renaming," *The Book of Occasional Services* (New York: Church Publishing, 2018), 120–24.

For younger children

SAY: Water is important in the Bible, it was important to Jesus and it is important in our lives. Christians use water to baptize people. This is a way of celebrating that we are part of God's family. Baptism helps us remember how water gives us life.

DO: Wash your hands, take a drink, or play in water while you talk about baptism.

PRAY: Dear God, thank you for the ways that you show us your love and grace. Thank you for giving me a place to belong. Amen.

13

What Is Communion?

After Jesus had been teaching and healing people for a while, and right before he was arrested, he and his friends were sharing a meal. Jesus and his friends remembered how much God loves people when he prayed a blessing for their food and drink. First, he took some bread, said thank you to God for it, then told his friends, "Eat this bread; it is my body." Then he took some wine, said thank you to God for it, shared that with his friends, and said, "Drink this wine; it is my blood." Years later, the friends would eat and drink, pray and sing, and remember this time with Jesus, knowing that in a holy and mysterious way, he was still with them. (Retold from Luke 22)

Communion is something that most Christian churches do as part of their worship. Some churches call it "The Lord's Supper." Some call it "Eucharist." Some churches do this often, as much as every week or every day, and others less often. This ritual comes from the story of Jesus sharing a last meal with his friends before he died. It involves eating bread or a wafer and drinking wine or juice, along with praying and reading scripture, to remember that story and remember that Jesus is with us. We always have communion with others, not alone. It is about eating and being part of Jesus all together and doesn't make sense for just one person.

Spiritual Practice: **Have you ever had communion or seen other people pray and worship this way? What was it like? As you think about how you've seen** this in your church, draw a picture of what you see, or write the words that you remember from the prayer and worship.

Some churches use bread baked by people in the community or bought from the store, and some use wafers or crackers. Some churches use wine and others use juice. Most churches and communities will read or retell or pray parts of the story you read at the beginning of this chapter, about the first time this meal was shared by Jesus. It is special and important to say these ancient words as part of the ritual, remembering that we are connected to Jesus and his friends, so long and far ago, through the Holy Spirit. There are as many different ways to share in this prayer and ritual as there are different Christian churches and traditions, and all of these ways of worshipping God are good.

One common song that is sung as part of the communion service is "Let Us Break Bread Together." It is a kind of song called a "spiritual" that comes from the African American Christian tradition. Do you know that song?

Spiritual Practice: **You can learn it and sing it.**

Let us break bread together on our knees.
Let us break bread together on our knees.
When I fall on my knees with my face to the rising sun,
O Lord, have mercy on me.

Let us drink wine together on our knees.
Let us drink wine together on our knees.
When I fall on my knees with my face to the rising sun,
O Lord, have mercy on me.

Christians participate in communion as a way of being connected to Jesus, his life and death and resurrection. But because of Jesus's own Jewish religion and identity, the ritual of communion also connects us to generations of people who eat a sacred meal in connection to their community and God, remembering God's loving presence and powerful liberation in their lives. It makes a lot of sense that one of the last things

that Jesus did with his friends was share a meal, because we know that sharing food with others was so important to him. After all, he loved to go to weddings and dinner parties, and he fed thousands of people as part of his ministry and work.

There is something essential and important about sharing food and drink as part of how we worship God and connect as a community of faith. Food and drink nourish our bodies and give us energy so that we can live and move, work and play, feel and think. What we eat and drink becomes a part of our bodies, as our digestive system processes the nutrients and moisture throughout our bodies. This is necessary to our survival, and by eating and drinking as part of worship, we remember this and remember that eating and drinking are sacred.

We remember that God is the Creator and Sustainer of all life any time we nourish our bodies, even when it's not at church! Whenever we gather with other people to prepare or share a meal, we are honoring the gifts of food and drink to our bodies, but we are also doing what Jesus showed us: eating together! At the last meal Jesus shared with his friends before he died, he told them to follow his example by repeating the ritual of the bread and the cup after he was gone. You can remember God's gifts that sustain our lives and Jesus's invitation to remember him any time and any place you eat with others.

What is it like when you gather to share food with others?
What special meals do you share with people you love?
How do you feel when you share food together?

Have you ever lost electricity and not been able to cook food in your kitchen, or had a time when your family needed groceries? Have you ever gone through a hard time and someone brought you or your family food, or have you ever taken a meal to someone else who you knew was having a hard time? Having good, warm food to eat is so important for our bodies to be healthy, and sharing food with others is so important for our families, churches, and communities.

Justice Story ~ **There's an organization called Meals on Wheels that helps make sure people who need warm food to eat can get warm meals. This group started long ago during World War II, when many homes had been damaged, many people did not have much money, and people were sad and tired. Folks in those situations were not always able to get and prepare their own food. Neighbors and volunteer groups worked together to make meals and deliver them so that everyone would have enough. The work of Meals on Wheels continues now as an organization in many different communities across the planet, getting food to those who need it. The Meals on Wheels group in Portland, Oregon, was started by three women named Jean Wade, Martha Shull, and Cay Kreiger, who had noticed that some elderly people in their city had a difficult time going to the store, purchasing and preparing food for themselves. Jean, Martha, and Cay had also heard about Meals on Wheels, a way of getting food to hungry folks, and decided that might be a solution for the hungry people around them. In 1970, they started by feeding**

one dozen hungry people. Their dream grew and grew, and now Meals on Wheels People in Portland gives out 40,000 meals every week! That's a lot of meals!

Spiritual Practice: **Plan to share food with someone. You may be able to do this today, or arrange this for a later time. It might be preparing a snack for someone in your home or preparing a meal for a friend or neighbor.**

Perhaps you can volunteer with food-sharing work through your church, school, or neighborhood. Talk to an adult about what this might look like for you.

When the earliest Christians, friends and disciples of Jesus, became what we understand to be the church, they ate a whole big meal as part of their communion ritual and worship together. We know about this because the apostle Paul wrote to a church in a place called Corinth, in Greece, giving them instructions about how to be together at this meal. Unfortunately, even though the church community was gathering for a shared meal in their worship, they were treating each other badly. People who were so wealthy that they did not work, or had work that was more flexible, would arrive and begin to eat before everyone had gathered. Working folks, who could not come early, would arrive late, when all the food had already been eaten. Paul wrote that by acting this way, the wealthy people were hurting and embarrassing poorer members of their community and forgetting the entire purpose of sharing their meal.

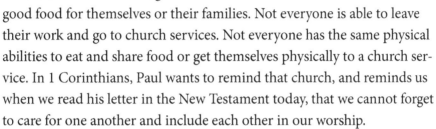

We know that not everyone has the same resources to get good food for themselves or their families. Not everyone is able to leave their work and go to church services. Not everyone has the same physical abilities to eat and share food or get themselves physically to a church service. In 1 Corinthians, Paul wants to remind that church, and reminds us when we read his letter in the New Testament today, that we cannot forget to care for one another and include each other in our worship.

When we eat and drink together in our communion worship and prayers, we are reminded of two important things. First, we remember that everyone has a place at God's table no matter what. Second, we remember those who might not have food to eat each day and do our part to help our church and larger community become places where everyone's needs are met.

For younger children

SAY: Communion is a way that Christians remember the story of how Jesus shared a meal with his friends. Whenever we eat and drink, around our table or God's table, we know that God's love is as close to us as the food and drink in our bellies.

DO: Invite children to help prepare food to share with others.

PRAY: Dear God, thank you for feeding me with love. Amen.

14
What Happens When We Die?

At the end of his life, Moses left the plains of Moab and went up to a high place on Mount Nebo, and God showed him the land. Moses saw far and wide, from Gilead to the Western Sea and the valley of Jericho. God told Moses, "I promised I would grant your descendants a home in this land. Now you see it with your own eyes, but you won't live long enough to cross into it." Then Moses, a devoted servant of God, died there in Moab. His family and community buried him there and mourned him for thirty days. (Retold from Deuteronomy 34)

When human bodies stop working, we die. Just like being born, death happens to everyone. When we die, our hearts stop beating and our brain stops making connections and our lungs stop breathing. Our bodies shut down.

Some people live a long, long time and their bodies slow down until eventually they die. Sometimes people get into accidents and are injured in a way that causes the body's systems of nourishment, breath, and connection to stop working earlier. Sometimes people get sick, and an illness makes it hard for their body to heal itself. Sometimes even doctors don't understand why someone's body shuts down.

What do you know about death? What questions do you have?
Talk with someone you trust about your questions.

Death is something that happens to our human bodies. But we are more than our bodies, so what happens to our souls, or our spirits or our love? No one knows for sure what happens to our souls when we die. People from all times, places, cultures, and religions have asked this question and have wondered about what happens next. Every religious tradition and every culture across space and time has their own ideas about what happens after death. But only people who have died have experienced what happens after.

The people who wrote the Bible had a lot to say about what happens when we die. Some of the ancient Old Testament writings say that when humans die, they return to the soil from which God created them and their spirit goes back to God (Ecclesiastes 12:7). Death completes the full circle of life, from God forming humans from the dust of the ground (Genesis 2) to the human body returning to the ground after death.

In the New Testament, the writers of the Epistles (the letters to the Romans, Corinthians, Ephesians, etc.) tried to understand what Jesus meant when he said, "Whoever believes in me will not die but have life everlasting" (John 11:26). These writers talked about death as something to be defeated. To them, Jesus was the person who showed us how to overcome death by sharing our love with the world.

People who study science also help us understand what happens when we die. Here on earth, we can observe the natural process of death and decay every day. When leaves fall or an animal dies or a tree is cut down, the molecules that make up those things go back into the earth. Those molecules get made into new combinations, so they are not wasted when

something dies. Energy is another thing that is not wasted: it is always coming from someplace and going somewhere. Energy can be transferred from person to person to animal to plant to the ground to the air. Energy cannot be created or destroyed. When someone dies, the energy from their bodies continues forever.

Justice Story ~ **In Genesis 3:19, God says that humans come from the dust of the ground and will return to the ground when they die. Some groups of people work together to provide space where people's bodies can be buried in environmentally friendly ways, also called "green burial." These places are part of a movement called "conservation burial," where part of the land is a nature-friendly cemetery with no plastics, metals, or concrete used in the burial process. The rest of the land is cared for by local naturalists and conservationists who work to preserve the local species of plants, animals, and insects. Amy Cunningham is a funeral director, a person whose job is to prepare bodies to be buried and work with families whose loved one has died. Amy lives in Brooklyn, New York, and she works with green burial. In this work, Amy brings together her love of people, nature, and the mystery of life and death, and helps people make decisions about their bodies after they die that will honor the earth we live in. ~**

Spiritual Practice: **Everything in nature, from the molecules that make up our bodies to the energy that makes us live, is recycled. Nothing is ever wasted. Find items around your house that you would normally throw away or recycle. How else could you use the items? Create some art with whatever you have!**

Death can seem like a big mystery. And in some ways, it is! We can't easily observe what happens to a person's soul or spirit. Throughout our lives we learn that there are some things beyond what we can sense and understand, and what happens to our souls when we die might be one of those things.

Some Christians talk about people "going to heaven" after death. That idea doesn't come from the Bible. Even Jesus never talked about "going to heaven." Instead, in the Old Testament, the ancient Hebrew prophets talked about a time when God would come to earth, offering healing to people and to the whole of Creation. During Jesus's lifetime, his followers thought about Jesus as God come to dwell on earth as promised. The "kingdom of God" and the "kingdom of heaven" that Jesus talked about were more about a way of living in harmony with other people and God's Creation instead of a physical place someone will go when they die.

After Jesus's time, the people who wrote the books included in the New Testament looked forward to Jesus returning to earth and making all relationships right with God. One of these books, Revelation, describes a vision of a time when good will be victorious against evil and when God will bring God's kingdom to earth. In Revelation 21:4, the writer says that God "will wipe every tear from their eyes. Death will be no more." Much art and music and literature has been inspired by this book of the Bible, some of the ideas and images becoming so popular that people forget Jesus didn't talk about going to heaven after death. Jesus does say that

after death, people who do God's will of living with justice and love will be reunited with God (Matthew 25:31–46). He even imagined that God has a big house with so many rooms in it that everyone has a place to live (John 14:2).

What do you imagine heaven could be like?
How do you imagine God's kingdom on earth would feel?
What do you wonder about heaven?

It's okay not to have an answer about what happens to our souls when we die. Or, if we do have an idea of an answer, it's okay not to understand it right away.

Because we do know lots of things about God from the Bible and from our lived experiences. We know that God is with us through Jesus, who is called Emmanuel, which means "God is with us" (Matthew 1:23). We know that God's love offers comfort even in the most difficult times (Psalm 23). We know that God's love is more powerful and everlasting than anything human or divine (Romans 8:38–39).

Spiritual Practice: **At the dinner table or before you go to bed, light a candle with an adult. If you know someone who has died, say their name and a short prayer: "Loving God, thank you for giving us _____ to know and love." The light of the candle reminds us of that person's love shining in our lives.**

Love does not end when someone dies. You may be reminded of that person's love for you in a bird chirping on a branch or a photo of them or something special they gave you. When you love someone and they die, your love continues, too. You can use your love for that person as you grieve them by doing something that person loved. Some people find it helpful to spend time with others mourning that person. It's healthy to talk about the person who has died, to say their name aloud and remember that person's life.

How do you know that someone loves you, even after they die?
What can you do to remember love after someone dies?

When someone we love dies, our pain is real. Our hearts hurt. They may even feel like breaking. We might not want to do normal things in our everyday lives, because our lives aren't normal anymore. When Moses died, his friends and family and the whole community cried and talked about him and made time to feel sad for a whole month! Even after those 30 days, there were probably moments, even days and weeks, when the people missed Moses terribly. After someone dies, we must learn how to live without that loved one. Living is courageous, especially when we hurt so deeply because we miss someone who is gone.

When a person dies, sometimes people can say things that don't make sense. They might say, "It's all in God's plan" or "They're in a better place" or "They're just sleeping." The people who say these things are trying to offer comfort and show they care, but the words they use can be confusing or upsetting or even just plain wrong. It's important to talk to people we love around us when someone dies, even (and especially) when we are confused about what people are saying.

When a life ends, the people who are left behind often will want to remember it in some way. Whether it is a beloved pet or a grandparent or a church member or a friend, marking the memory of someone can be helpful. You can speak someone's name aloud and tell stories about them. You can thank God for giving them to us to know and love, and to love us.

For younger children

SAY: Death is a big mystery. When we die, our bodies stop working and our spirits go with God. It's okay not to understand how that happens. We can trust that God's love is always with us and holding us after we die.

DO: Light a candle and talk about someone you love who has died.

PRAY: Dear God, thank you for love that is even bigger than death. Thank you for always being with me. Amen.

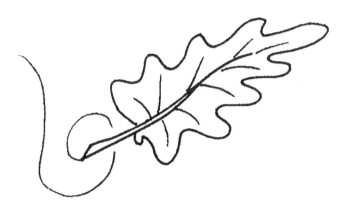

15
What Is a Saint?

Jesus liked to have plenty of quiet time to pray and talk with God. That's when he prayed and rested. Once, he went away to a mountain to pray and be quiet, and invited his friends Peter, James, and John to join him. Suddenly, Jesus started to change. His face shined like the sun and even his clothing changed to look bright white! But that's not all! Suddenly, Moses and Elijah, two prophets and great leaders of Israel who had died many, many generations ago, were also there, having a conversation with Jesus. Peter and James and John were so amazed, they didn't know what to do! Then a cloud covered the mountain and God's voice said, "This is my son. I love him and I am proud of him. Listen to him!" (Retold from Matthew 17:1–8)

What is a saint? Is this a word you have heard in your church or community? What are saints like? Who or what do you think of when you hear the word "saint"?

A saint is someone who gives us an example of living full of God's love. "Saint" with a capital "S" means a person who has been officially recognized by the church as a special person whose life showed us something important about God. Sometimes the word "saint" is used to talk about a person whose life points other people to God through their goodness, love, honesty, or courage.

The Bible is full of these people, both big-S Saints and little-s saints. Their stories and lives show us important things about God and how they tried to live according to God's love and guidance. We know that Jesus certainly showed us God in a special way; we believe he was God's son! His birth, life, work of healing and teaching, and his death and resurrection are the most important ways that Christians understand God. But other biblical characters, even the most complicated ones and the ones who made bad choices, also show us glimpses of God, teach us important lessons, and remind us of all the ways that we can love God and other people.

The biblical letter to the Hebrews calls this the "cloud of witnesses," and the Apostle's Creed refers to the "communion of saints." Both phrases remind us that we are connected to countless people who have loved God with their whole life and heart. You could imagine these people standing on a balcony or sitting in stadium seats looking out over your life and cheering for you. We are part of a family of faithful people that extends beyond time and place and offers us encouragement along the way.

In the story of Jesus on the mountain, we get a glimpse of one amazing way that people of faith in God are connected to each other. Most of all, we see how mysterious our connection to other people of God can be. When Jesus met God on that mountain, he was with his friends from the present moment: Peter, James, and John. But the four of them were not alone. Moses and Elijah, two of the most significant spiritual and social leaders of Israel, were there as well. How could that be? Were they really there on the mountain? Was it a vision or a dream? However it happened, it was a very real experience for Jesus and his friends. The proclamation of God over Jesus, celebrating who he was becoming, called for witnesses from the past. These spiritual heroes who had lived out God's power and love and made the way to freedom for God's people before were there as an affirmation and encouragement to Jesus.

We might never have a vision or experience of meeting someone from the past like this story, but we all have stories and a heart connection to people who have been important examples of faith and love to us. We can receive encouragement from their stories and witness.

Spiritual Practice: **If you were meeting God on a mountain, who would be with you? Imagine yourself into the Bible story with art. Draw a picture of yourself, a few friends or family members you**

know right now, and a few saints from the past who would be there to meet God with you.

Some traditions ask saints who have died to pray to God with and for them, asking for that person's faithfulness through the mysterious connection of all God's people across time and space. This way of praying with a saint usually connects the experience of the person praying with some story or quality of that saint.

For instance, traditions and stories about St. Francis of Assisi are connected to animals, nature, plants, and seasons. Francis was a friar from Italy who lived hundreds of years ago. Once, the story goes, Francis and

some of his friends were walking down a road when he noticed a flock of birds perched in the trees nearby. Francis thought they were beautiful and felt moved to preach a sermon to them. A sermon to birds! He walked over and, calling them "my sisters the birds," told them that God had given them beauty and freedom, and it was God who provided for them each day. Francis encouraged the birds to always be grateful and praise God, and the birds chirped and bobbed their heads in agreement.

Another story of this saint tells how a terrible wolf came to town. Francis told the wolf to stop hurting animals and scaring people, then scolded the wolf and called him to live in God's peace with the humans in the town. The wolf obeyed, and the townspeople fed the wolf from their own homes until he died. These special connections with animals are why some people go to church to bless their pets on St. Francis's Day, praying with Francis and honoring that his stories and faith are still alive with us today.

We might also think of saints as anyone, even people we know personally, who have been particularly loving, kind, or just, and who teach us about God. This includes people who have died and people who are still alive today.

Some cultures have special ways of remembering family members who have died, through family shrines, a ritual of visiting burial places, or a special display of photos or commemoration like an *ofrenda* for Día de los Muertos.

Our communities are also full of living saints, people who are loving, brave, and wise, and whose lives point us toward God. We might know them in our families or churches, at school or in community leadership, or from our neighborhoods.

When we think about those folks in the cloud of witnesses who are still alive, we honor them by listening to their wisdom and following their examples, asking them questions or praying with them, and thanking them and God for the ways that they show God's love in the world.

Spiritual Practice: **Do you have a friend, family member, teacher, or neighbor who teaches you a lot about God and God's love? How do they teach you? Write them a note, draw them a picture, or call them on the phone to share your appreciation for teaching you about God.**

We also celebrate as a larger community or society those legacies of people who have died who have had a big impact in the world. Their lives become a witness for our own hopes and struggles to make the world a better place.

Justice Story ~ *Anywhere in the world, you can find helpers supporting friends and neighbors in need. When people can't get access to basic necessities like food, clean water, housing, clothing, and education, helpers step in not just to provide these things but also to advocate for more access for those in need. Auntie Na's Village on the west side of Detroit is a stronghold in the community, offering after-school tutoring, free meals, youth employment, support for unhoused neighbors, and farm-fresh meals. Auntie Na is not just the name of an organization; she is a real person! She has lived in her neighborhood for her entire life, and grew up with her grandparents, who took in children to get them safely off the streets. Na's family worked hard to help their neighborhood weather the challenges of urban decay, foreclosure, drug epidemics, financial collapse, government crackdown, school bankruptcy, and more, and so as Auntie Na grew up, she joined her community's and family's work of caring for one another. Today,*

Auntie Na's Village has purchased several vacant lots and foreclosed homes in the neighborhood, transforming them into community outreach centers, urban gardens, and a community park. The outreach centers include Medical, Nutrition, Clothing, and Learning Houses, and the Village has dreams of expanding to a Mercy house to support survivors of domestic violence. Auntie Na's Village is a place of radical hospitality, where all are welcomed and loved.

Spiritual Practice: Think of a Saint or a saint that you would like to learn more about. This might be someone officially recognized by the church, someone who made a big impact on the world, or someone you know. Look them up on the internet, check out a library book about them, or ask them about their life. Find out something new, and offer a simple prayer of thanks, like this:
"Dear God, thank you for _____.
Thank you for the ways that they teach me to _____."

For younger children

SAY: A saint is a person who shows us God's love in important ways. Saints are ordinary people like me and you. They listened to the Holy Spirit and followed the teachings of Jesus. We can learn more about God when we learn about God's saints.

DO: Think of a friend, family member, teacher, or neighbor who teaches you about God and shares God's love.

PRAY: Dear God, thank you for loving and faithful people, and for all they can teach me about you. Amen.

16

What Is Sin? What Is Forgiveness?

Jonah was a prophet who spoke for God. One day God told Jonah that he should go to the city of Nineveh and tell them to change their hearts and minds to follow God. Jonah didn't like the people of Nineveh, so he didn't want to go. Instead of listening to God's call, Jonah turned the opposite way and tried to hide from God by getting on a boat and going out to sea. While he was on the boat, a great storm came and all the sailors were scared. They thought the storm was happening because God was upset at someone on the boat. The sailors threw Jonah off the boat and into the sea and he was swallowed by a gigantic fish. While he was in the belly of the fish, Jonah thought about his choice to run away from God's call. He said sorry to God. The fish spat him out onto dry land and Jonah tried again to be a prophet. God gave him a second chance. (Retold from Jonah 1–3)

When have you made a mistake? Have you ever made a choice that you knew would hurt someone or cause some trouble? What happened?

Humans are not perfect. We all make mistakes. We all cause harm. One word that we use to talk about a mean or hurtful choice or a harmful mistake is "sin." Sometimes we know we are doing something wrong or something that makes God sad. Sometimes we find out later that something we did was hurtful. Sometimes we don't even realize we are doing harm. Whatever mistake we make, it is important to remember that we can always learn to do better in the future. Learning and growing is part of being human, too. God loves and cares for us even when we make bad choices.

The prophet Jonah, whom we read about in the beginning of this chapter, sinned when he ran away from what God wanted him to do. He hid from God and lied to himself that he didn't have to do what God called him to do. Hiding from God was a bad choice. But God didn't leave Jonah, even when he ran away to sea and was swallowed by a great big fish! God was with Jonah, and God gave Jonah a second chance.

What is a choice you've made that made you feel good because you knew it was the right thing to do?

In the beginning of the story of Genesis, the first humans lived in the Garden of Eden, a beautiful place where they had everything they needed. God gave the humans guidelines to follow so that they would be safe and have healthy relationships. But the story tells us that one of the humans was tempted to ignore God's directions. The first humans ignored God's rules and did what they wanted to do. They thought that they knew more than God, and maybe that they could even be like God. When humans

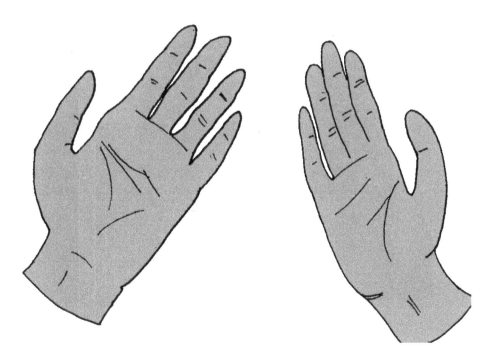

forget to let God be God and act like they know better than God, they hurt their relationship with God and that is called "sin." Every human sins, sometimes every day. It is part of being human.

Sometimes sin can feel like distance between you and another person, or you and God. Even when it feels like that, remember that God is a loving Creator and is with us all the time. God knows we can do better, but God never stops loving us. God's love in our lives teaches us how to live with justice and kindness.

All sins have consequences. Sometimes the consequences might be obvious, like when your grownups say that you need to apologize to a sibling. Other times the consequences can be serious, like when you have to give back something that you took, spend time in detention, or need to show a loved one they can trust you again. Society has laws that people made to try to make consequences for very serious sins like stealing, assault, and murder. But because humans can never know exactly what God wants or speak for God, sometimes those laws wind up hurting people, too.

Have you ever heard a story about when human-made laws hurt people? How are God's guidelines on how to live alike and different from the laws that humans make? How can you help make human laws more just?

Sin is not an end. If you make a bad choice, it does not mean you are a bad person. If you make a mistake, it does not mean you will always make mistakes and never do anything right. It does not mean that you do not deserve to have good things happen to you. It *never* means that God doesn't love you or that God leaves you behind. Humans can learn and do better so we can forgive and repair our relationships. The Bible is filled with stories about how humans sin and then learn to do better. Because all actions have consequences, the first humans had to leave the garden and live somewhere else.

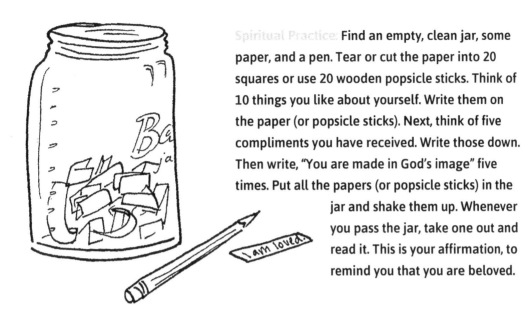

Spiritual Practice: Find an empty, clean jar, some paper, and a pen. Tear or cut the paper into 20 squares or use 20 wooden popsicle sticks. Think of 10 things you like about yourself. Write them on the paper (or popsicle sticks). Next, think of five compliments you have received. Write those down. Then write, "You are made in God's image" five times. Put all the papers (or popsicle sticks) in the jar and shake them up. Whenever you pass the jar, take one out and read it. This is your affirmation, to remind you that you are beloved.

Do you know what happened when the humans left the garden? God kept loving them and God kept caring for them. They lived in a new place and had to learn new ways of living, but God was with them the whole time. God continued to walk and talk with the humans and their descendants . . . and God still speaks with us today! No matter what we do, God forgives us every time we sin and return to God, like when God gave Jonah a second chance to follow God's call. God's love is what helps us learn to do better.

**Spiritual Practice: What does your body feel like when you make a mistake?
Who do you talk to when you have done something wrong?
How can you remind yourself, and other people, that God loves you all the time?**

When we think about sin and mistakes, we also always think about forgiveness, or how we can grow, change, and make things right. Anyone who has ever said "I'm sorry" knows that is easier to think about than to do! Apologizing and making things right can feel scary and make us vulnerable. It can give us tangled-up feelings in our bellies and make our hearts beat harder or faster. But when we mess up, we can receive God's forgiveness and ask for others' forgiveness, too.

Here is what a good apology needs. First, we say exactly what we did that was wrong and take responsibility for our actions, words, or choices. Then we do what we can to make a situation right. If we broke something, we might need to fix it or replace it. If we told an untrue story, we need to tell the whole truth. If we said unkind words, we need to say kind ones. If we took something, we need to give it back. Finally, we change our actions, words, and choices in the future. We commit ourselves to doing things differently next time and follow through.

When have you needed to apologize and receive forgiveness? What happened? When has someone else apologized and asked for your forgiveness? What happened?

Justice Story ~ *When God invites us to offer forgiveness and ask for forgiveness, it can be hard to know what that might look like when the hurts are very big. How can we love one another again? How can we make things right? One group of people in Concord, Massachusetts, were asking these questions about crime and justice in their community. They started a group called Communities for Restorative Justice, a partnership between the community members and the criminal justice system.*

The phrase "restorative justice" means that instead of punishing someone for a bad choice or mistake, there are steps the whole community can take to make things right and heal hurt places. This can protect people who made bad choices from harsh consequences that don't help them grow, and instead invite them to make things right with the people they have hurt. Communities for Restorative Justice brings together people who have committed a crime and people who have been hurt by that crime, along with people who can help them talk through what has happened and figure out what should happen next. One time, a woman in the Concord community went swimming and left her clothes and belongings on the shore. When she got back from the water, she saw that her clothes were thrown around and her wallet was stolen, including money she needed to feed her family! She called for help from other people nearby and called the police. Soon, three girls were found to be responsible for the theft and admitted their wrong actions. Instead of having these girls charged with their crime, the woman met with them and talked to them about how embarrassed, hurt, and angry their actions made her feel. They all apologized to the person they had wronged and agreed to serve in their community as a way of making things right. Concord's practice of forgiveness through restorative justice has changed the lives of these women and many others by finding new ways to apologize, ask for and offer forgiveness, and heal their community.

For younger children

SAY: Everyone sins and makes mistakes. God never stops loving us, even when we do something wrong. Forgiveness is making things right, a way that we offer kindness when someone's done something wrong and accept responsibility when we have hurt someone else.

DO: Remember a time you made a wrong choice that caused trouble. Remember a time you made a good choice and felt proud.

PRAY: Dear God, thank you for always giving us a chance to make things right and to grow. Amen.

17

How Do We Care for Each Other?

One day not long after David became the king of Israel, he was thinking about the family and friends of Saul, the king who had gone before him. David and Saul had been friends, and David had also been good friends with Saul's son, Jonathan. But David and Saul had disagreements. Saul became jealous and was unkind to David, and they became enemies. Even though their friendship had gone wrong, David wondered if there were any of Saul's friends or family members to whom he should show kindness to try and make things right.

David found out about a young man named Mephibosheth, Saul's grandson. Mephibosheth had a physical disability of movement because of an injury to his feet and legs when he was young. In this time and culture where the economy was all about farming, it was difficult for him to earn a living and provide for his family. David visited with Mephibosheth and told him, "I want to give you everything that belonged to your grandfather when he was king so that you can be well and take care of your family. I want to be your friend and share my home and meals with you. I want us to be like family because I loved your father and your grandfather." (Retold from 2 Samuel 9)

In both the Old Testament and the New Testament, God tells God's people that the two greatest commands, the most important things for them to do, are to love God and love each other. We show our love for God in worship and prayer, and we also love God when we love other people.

What do you think of when you hear the word "love"? Close your eyes and imagine the face of someone it is easy for you to love, someone who makes you happy. Offer a love prayer for them like this: "May you be healthy; may you be happy; may you know you are loved."

Then think of someone who isn't hard or easy to love, someone you don't know well.

Offer a love prayer for them, too: "May you be healthy; may you be happy; may you know you are loved."

Now think about someone who is really frustrating or who has been unkind.

Even if this is someone you don't have a good relationship with, or a person it is not safe for you to be with, see whether you can pray for them: "May you be healthy; may you be happy; may you know you are loved."

Finally, imagine your own face. Touch your hands to your cheeks or wrap your arms around yourself in a big hug. Pray for and bless yourself: "May I be healthy; may I be happy; may I know I am loved."

When we love God and love other people, sometimes that love is a good feeling of being connected to each other, feeling happy and liking someone and wanting to be together. But the way God teaches us to love each other is more than just a good feeling. This love is also expressed and experienced by taking care of others, putting that feeling into action, and acting in a loving way even when the feeling isn't there. We start to practice this kind of love when we pray for and send loving attitudes toward others that we really enjoy, those we don't know at all, even people we don't particularly like, and especially toward ourselves. We practice love all around, in hard and easy ways, so that when we don't feel like love, we still know how.

When have you shown love to someone, even when you didn't feel loving?

The Bible tells us over and over, through so many stories and lessons, to love each other. It can be hard work to love all the time, and we need reminders. It can also be tricky to know exactly what love looks like, since making a choice for love can be lots of different things, in different situations, for different people.

In the story of King David and Mephibosheth, David wanted to put his love for Jonathan and Saul into action by doing something good for their relatives. David expressed his love for this family through his words to Mephibosheth, but even more through his actions. He showed welcome, kindness, and respect. He took care of Mephibosheth's physical needs and became his friend.

The Bible and Christian tradition also teach that love is more than the care that we show just one person. God asks us to bring love into every aspect of our life, work, and community. The Old Testament gives many instructions about how to think about caring for other people on a bigger

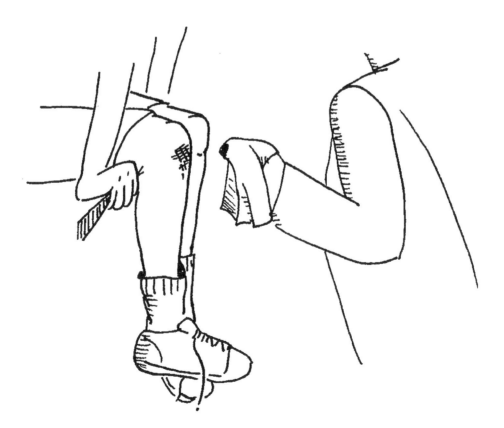

scale. From how we farm to how we pray, honor Sabbath and rest, welcome strangers, and provide for people who need help, there are many suggestions, guidelines, and stories to show us how. Jesus also cares a lot about making our love bigger for the whole society and told many parables, or wisdom stories, about how we might do that.

One parable, or story, that Jesus told was about a man who owned a farm, who went into town to hire people to work for him. Early in the morning, he hired some workers for a good day's pay. Later in the morning, and then at lunchtime, he went back and hired some more. That afternoon, he decided he needed more help, and even again toward the very end of the workday he still needed more. Each time he went, people were waiting, hoping for a job to come so that they could work to earn money. In the evening, when the work was complete, the farm owner paid every person a full day's wage, no matter how long they worked. When the ones who worked all day long complained, the farm owner said he could be generous if he wanted. This story shows that even people who don't have enough work or fair work should still have their needs met, and that generosity in our money and business is important.

What do you think about that story? Was it fair? Where was love in that story?

The farm owner showed care through his generosity. This care wasn't in the context of a friendship or a personal connection, but about going above and beyond what was necessary and choosing to be good to someone with less power, money, and influence.

This is just one example of how Jesus taught us to practice care and love in our communities. Throughout the stories about Jesus's life, he shows how important it is to show this kind of care to everyone, through kindness, but also through justice. Justice is setting things right in the way our society and world works, so that all people can flourish.

Spiritual Practice: **Take a piece of paper and draw four big circles on it. In the first circle, draw pictures or write the names of people in your family or home that you love. Draw or write how you love them.**

In the second circle, draw pictures or write the names of your friends. Draw or write how you love them.

In the third circle, draw pictures or write the names of people who are in your community, perhaps in your school, church, or neighborhood. Draw or write how you love them.

In the fourth circle, draw pictures or write the names of people (or a description if you don't know a name) who are in your larger community, who you might not know or ever meet. Draw or write how you love them.

Justice Story ~ One great example of a place where people are caring for each other with kindness and love but also through justice is an organization called Thistle Farms in Nashville, Tennessee. In 1997, Rev. Becca Stevens opened a home for women to be safe, heal, and grow after they have gone through a particularly hard time, like being in prison, being hurt by a partner or family member, or getting well after having troubles with addiction. After a few years in the home, the women were doing well in their journey to recovery, but they faced challenges with finding jobs and saving money to live well. Becca saw these challenges, so she and

the women and some other volunteers began making candles and selling them. Today, Thistle Farms serves many women who are recovering from tough times and who are gaining job skills and financial stability. Their motto is "love heals," and the community offers love, celebration, kindness, and a safe home for the women in the program. But kindness and love need the supportive structures of justice to flourish. Thistle Farms started businesses of a café and store so that the women in the community also have good jobs and can make money. They make soaps, lotions, and candles to sell that are good for bodies and good for the earth. Community members travel the country talking about their work and love, so that other people might be inspired to care for others through kindness, love, and justice wherever they might be.

That vision of caring for others with different life stories and sharing ideas of caring across the world is important for Christians, because we are taught to care even for the people who are most different from us. The apostle Paul, one of the earliest leaders in the church, was committed to teaching people to love each other, to really care in big and small ways, no matter what. For people who love God, he wrote, "There is no longer Jew or Greek, there is no longer slave or free, there is no longer male and female; for all of you are one in Christ Jesus" (Galatians 3:28). While we might not be familiar with the categories of difference Paul wrote about, we certainly find diversity in our communities.

What are some of the ways we think about difference today? What's one way that you are loving and connected to people who are different from you?

Even the ways that we think we might be most different from each other can't separate us from loving each other. That's why Christians are called to show loving kindness and practical care for all people, no matter their citizenship, their body or intellectual ability, their gender or race; no matter how much money they have, whom they love, where they live, or what cultural practices they have or religious beliefs they hold.

When we think about this kind of love for people who are different from us, people who we may not even know, we might like to revisit the story of the Good Samaritan in Luke 10:25–37. This was one of Jesus's most important teaching stories, called parables, because it reminds us that every person in the world is our neighbor, and we are called to love anyone who crosses our paths.

For younger children

SAY: Jesus taught us to love each other, but love is more than just a feeling. We love others by taking care of them, treating them fairly, and remembering that we are all loved by God.

DO: Learn and practice part of the love mediation: "May you be healthy; may you be happy; may you know you are loved," and "May I be healthy; may I be happy; may I know I am loved."

PRAY: God, help me grow in love and care for myself and others. Amen.

18
How Do We Care for Creation?

God saw all of Creation and called it "good." (Retold from Genesis 1)

The earth is made of the all-encompassing love of God. The heavens were created by God's spoken word and all that dwell in the heavens created by the breath of God. (Retold from Psalm 33:5–6)

In Genesis 1, God created everything and called it good. Humans are part of this good Creation. All of Creation was made in God's image, from the butterflies to the whales to you and me. In the beginning of the Bible, God told humans to care for the Creation. The book of Genesis tells us that the first humans named all of the creatures and tended God's garden. As the human population grew and spread out all over the land, God gave people more directions about how to be good caretakers.

Sometimes humans treat the world around us like we exist outside of it, but we don't. We are part of Creation, just like the rocks that make up the mountains and the grasses growing on the plains, and the birds that migrate south for the winter. The land affects us, and we affect the land. God's dream is for all Creation to live in harmony together.

Spiritual Practice: **What can we do to live in harmony with each other and nature? How are you a part of Creation?**

When Moses gave God's people the guidelines showing the way to live with justice and peace, caring for the earth was included. Exodus 23 describes how people should not overwork the land by farming too much. Every seven days and every seven years, people should stop working and rest, and they should let the land rest, too! God's people would have enough food to sustain themselves, their families and neighbors and animals because of how well the land provided in the first six years. In that seventh year, all the extra produce from the land should be left in the fields so that those who were experiencing poverty and the wild animals would also have something to eat. These same rules are expanded in Leviticus 25, getting more and more specific about how humans are to treat each other in these "sabbath years," also called "jubilee." God's good Creation needs rest and care.

Think about a place that is meaningful to you. What plants and creatures live there? How do you take care of that place?

Indigenous people are people who have lived in partnership with the land for thousands of years and are native to that land. There are indigenous peoples all over the world. To many indigenous peoples, the earth is not a resource to be used but a living being that must be cared for. In nearly every indigenous culture, rituals and ceremonies mark the passage of time and how the seasons affect humans. Indigenous peoples across time and space have taken great care of the natural resources where they live, careful not to use too much of something or put too much stress on the place where they live. All humans can learn a lot about how to care for the earth by learning from indigenous peoples and honoring indigenous wisdom and practices.

Which people groups are indigenous to the place you call home? How can you learn about these neighbors, their histories and traditions?

Over time, some people forgot how to live close to the land and treat it well. They read the stories in the Bible about taking care of the land and thought that it meant that people could use the Creation all they wanted. Sometimes they farmed so much that the land couldn't rest. Sometimes they cut down all the trees or caught so many fish or hunted so many bison that the natural processes of growth couldn't recover. Sometimes the people changed the shape of the land so much that the water didn't have a clear path to travel anymore, resulting in dams and flooding that hurt people and damaged communities. When people think about the earth only as something to be used, they don't always make healthy decisions.

What are some healthy decisions people can make to care for the earth? What are some unhealthy decisions people make that impact the planet?

Justice Story ~ **In the 1970s, women in rural Kenya noticed that streams were drying up, they were having difficulty maintaining crops, and they needed to walk longer distances to find fuel. The National Council of Women of Kenya, led by Professor Wangari Maathai, listened to these women. The Green Belt Movement was founded to help the women plant trees that would store rainwater, provide food and firewood, and bind the soil to prevent its breakdown from wind and rain. This work would also bring some profit to the women. Over time, Professor Maathai recognized that the problems affecting poor communities were deeply intertwined with environmental issues. The Green Belt Movement began offering environmental education classes that included political and economic empowerment. People who participated in these classes dedicated themselves to working together for the good of their whole community, including the environment. They asked political leaders to listen to the people and advocate for their needs, such as having representation in decision making about how land is used for agriculture, forestry, and fuel. Professor Maathai's work was honored by the Nobel Peace Prize, and since the Green Belt Movement was founded, more than 40 million trees have been planted across**

Kenya, mostly by women. This effort has encouraged people all around the world to come together to plant trees, a simple vision of care for our common home. ～

In the New Testament, Romans 8 says the Creation groans while waiting for justice. Today, one of the biggest justice issues is climate change. Over the billions of years the earth has existed, the climate has shifted many times, warming and cooling over and over again. These are natural processes that happen over time. Climate change is happening right now. But this kind of climate change is different from other times in the earth's history because the change is happening faster because of human activity, like fossil fuel-powered electricity, industry and manufacturing, cars and airplanes, and even raising livestock. All these processes are releasing dangerous chemicals into the air that make the earth warmer. Increasing temperatures are making polar ice melt, ocean levels rise, stronger storms, and droughts that affect not only human lives but also the lives of plants and animals. As the climate changes, some plants, animals, and insects cannot adapt and go extinct. We are seeing these extinctions happening right in front of us.

How do you observe the climate changing where you live? What do you wonder about climate change?

Today, we study some of these natural processes through science. We can use our brains to learn about the world around us and make the world a better/healthier place. Scientists have taught us that energy is never wasted, always moving through what is alive and creating new things, never created or destroyed. In nature, things we observe that appear dead and decaying are recycled by natural processes, and life begins again in a different way. For example, nurse logs in the forest are parts of trees that have fallen over and started to decompose on the ground. But their job is not finished just because they fall. Smaller trees and other plants and fungi begin growing out of this log, using the energy that the nurse log is giving off as it decomposes. Nature wastes nothing.

Spiritual Practice: **Find a place where you can observe nature. Make your body comfortable. Use your senses to observe your surroundings. What do you see? Hear? Smell? Feel? What animals are nearby? What plants? Spend some time breathing deep, full breaths as you honor God's creation. Remember, you are a part of Creation, too.**

From science, we learn that all the atoms in the universe, the building blocks that make up all things, are being recycled and rebuilt all the time, just like we might use LEGO blocks to build different creations at different times. Our bodies are a part of this process, too! The atoms that make our hearts and brains and elbows and bellybuttons are the same ones that made up stars and planets long ago. God created you out of the same atoms as stars. We can understand these scientific processes as part of God's good Creation. We can care for creation by paying attention to this one small way that God expresses God's never-ending love for us cycling through all the atoms in the cosmos.

As humans, we can make healthy choices to care for Creation. We can reduce the amount of stuff we buy. We can choose to reuse items in our homes, schools, and churches, making them useful for longer. We can choose to recycle, so that something new can be made from something old. We can remember that we are part of Creation and that the decisions

we make every day affect other humans and the world around us. Every person, young and old and in between, can choose to be a Creation caretaker, learning about their environment and how to keep it healthy.

What do you reuse or recycle? How does your family care for the planet? How can you encourage others to take care of their small corner of creation?

For younger children

SAY: God asks people to work together to protect nature and all the living things God has made. We can take care of creation by keeping the earth clean and not using more water and resources than we need.

DO: Go on a nature walk and explore!

PRAY: God, thank you for this beautiful earth and all the things you have made. Help me take care of it well. Amen.

19

What Is the Kingdom of God?

Jesus said, "The kingdom of God is like . . ."

Yeast added to a dough mixture, a bit of hope and love that can change its whole environment into a nourishing loaf of bread. (Retold from Matthew 13:32)

A tiny mustard seed that grew and grew and grew so big that it became a home for all the birds. One little seed's potential can create hospitality for all. (Retold from Matthew 13:31)

A pearl that was so precious and rare that it was worth selling everything to have it. (Retold from Matthew 13:45–46)

I am making a new heaven and a new earth. A special kingdom where there will be joy and delight. People will live whole, good lives. Everyone will have homes. Everyone will have enough food and water to sustain them. Everyone will be treated well at work. No one will be exploited or pushed down to lift another up. The wolf and the lamb will live side by side and the lion will eat grass like an ox. No one will be hurt, and nothing will be destroyed upon my holy mountain. (Retold from Isaiah 65)

The kingdom of God is not like any kingdoms or countries we have on earth. There is no geographical location where you can go to find it. The kingdom of God is a spiritual place, where people live with God's love, peace, and justice.

People have been wondering and thinking and writing about the kingdom of God for a long, long time. Some people thought that the kingdom of God would come when Jesus returns to earth at the end of time. They thought that to make the kingdom of God present on earth, God would have to judge the good people from the bad people so only the good people remain. But we all sometimes do good, healthy things and sometimes make bad choices or mistakes, and so the people decided that wasn't quite right. Other people thought that the kingdom of God was in the sky,

a heavenly place, and that when humans die, our spirits go up to heaven. And some people still think that the kingdom of God is something all of us are invited to create together: each day, by being your true self and living your life by helping others, you are helping to create the kingdom of God on earth.

Spiritual Practice: What have you heard about the kingdom of God? What do you picture when you imagine the kingdom of God? Look up some of the Bible stories referenced at the beginning of this chapter. Pick one to read aloud with a family member or friend. Using whatever art supplies you have, draw the kingdom of God. Remember, the kingdom of God is justice and peace and joy—so let your creativity flow!

A prophet named Isaiah, whose writings we have in the book of Isaiah in the Old Testament, talked about a "peaceable kingdom." He wrote that in this peaceable kingdom, relationships would be restored, like a wolf snuggling up with a lamb and a lion that no longer eats meat but grass. Isaiah says, "They will not hurt or destroy on all my holy mountain, for the earth shall be full of the knowledge of the Lord as the waters cover the sea" (Isaiah 11:9). In the peaceable kingdom, children will lead elders with wisdom and creativity, and elders will listen to children. In the peaceable kingdom, relationships that have been broken will be healed, and all people and the planet will be safe.

Spiritual Practice: Find a quiet, comfy place to sit. Ask someone to read Isaiah 65 to you aloud, slowly and clearly. If you are comfortable, close your eyes while they read. Take a few slow, full breaths. Imagine yourself in the peaceable kingdom. What does peace look like to you? What does it feel like? What does it smell, taste, and sound like? Where are you? Are you sitting or lying down or standing? Who is with you in the peaceable kingdom? Is anything missing in the peaceable kingdom? What do you want to take with you from the peaceable kingdom?

As Jesus grew up in the Roman Empire, he saw some people with a lot of wealth and some people who were begging on the streets. He saw some people who could afford big houses and some people who were

healed
FORGIVEN
Peace

homeless. He saw some people who were sick and made to live on the edges of cities. Because he grew up knowing about Isaiah's peaceable kingdom, Jesus started wondering about a world with all relationships healed, between people and with the earth. This vision, which Jesus called the kingdom of God, gave people hope. People began following Jesus. They kept working for justice and peace for all people because they knew that living in the kingdom of God was possible. That dream is still alive today. Each of us can be a part of making the kingdom of God real.

What kinds of relationships could be healed in the peaceable kingdom? How can you live like the peaceable kingdom is here, now?

Some people who think about God, called "theologians," suggested that the word "kingdom" isn't quite the right word to describe how God wants the world to be. In a kingdom, a king or queen rules over all the other people. Throughout history, we have seen that kingdoms can be places where there is abuse and oppression, and where God's grace and mercy is not seen as important. These theologians suggest that we take the "g" out of "kingdom" and then we have "kin-dom." You might have heard the word "kin" in the wassail carol or as part of other words like "kinship" or "kindred." "Kin" means family. The theologians who suggest this language say this is a fuller representation of what a world that follows the Way of Jesus is like: family. And, as we know, no family is the same! When we say "kin-dom," we are saying that in a world following the Way of Jesus, everyone is treated like family. A "kin-dom" where all are welcome is beautiful because diversity is celebrated.

Who are your "kin"? How can you treat people so they know they are part of God's family?

When we pray the Lord's Prayer, we say "your kingdom come on earth as it is in heaven." By praying that, we are asking for God to help us make the kingdom of God a reality, even if only for a short time. In lots of times and places, followers of Jesus live, care for one another and creation, and create communities that try to live like the kingdom of God on earth. One of these communities is Koinonia Farm in Georgia, formed in the 1940s by a group of families committed to living with justice and peace, sharing everything like the first Christian communities in the book of Acts. The founding families sometimes would say that Koinonia was a "demonstration plot for the Kingdom of God,"* a place where people would live together with generosity and justice. When Koinonia was founded, they welcomed families of any race to live and work and worship together, even though that was not a popular decision in the racially segregated South. Over time, people at Koinonia were threatened, even having bullets fired at them and bombs set by white supremacists. Through it all, the community at the Farm held strong to their dedication to living following the Way of Jesus. They welcomed all people to have fellowship around the table. Over time, the good work of Koinonia spread as members of the Farm community founded Habitat for Humanity, which builds houses for low-income people, and Jubilee Partners, which supports refugees from across the world. Koinonia is still around today, offering a place of hospitality to all. ~

_____

* koinoniafarm.org

When we make choices to love God by loving our neighbor, we are making the peaceable kingdom happen right now. We can encourage our friends to be peaceful or grow food to share with our hungry neighbors. We can break down racism by treating all people equally, by being friends with people who are different from us, and by listening to each other's stories. We can speak up when mean comments are made and help each other learn how to treat each other with justice. We can advocate for our neighbors who don't have houses or who need to be paid fairly for their work.

What will you do to make the world more like the peaceable kingdom?

For younger children

SAY: God's kingdom is not a faraway place or country. God's kingdom is anywhere that people are caring for each other and bringing peace. God's kingdom is wherever people live like Jesus taught us.

DO: Draw a picture of God's kingdom.

PRAY: God, help me to be a part of your kingdom, to bring love and peace everywhere I go. Amen.

Acknowledgments

Thank you to our wise, encouraging, and fearless editor Wendy Claire Barrie, who said "Let's make it!" when we couldn't find a book that we needed for parenting and ministry. Your encouragement, questioning, advocacy, and confidence in our work have meant the world to us as we bring this project into being.

We are grateful for all those who participated in and supported our research. We are especially grateful to all those who participated in our listening groups, who shared their deepest questions, longings, and heart-wondering with us: Heather, Davi, Sarah, Caroline, Brittany, Michael, Kelly, Leah, Nathan, Dianna, Lauren, Victoria, Benjamin, Viola, and Anna.

Thank you to the Rev. Erica Saunders, the Rev. Davi Weasley, Molly Carnes, and Clara for conversations about affirming transgender people and theologies of baptism. Thank you to Matthew Groves for offering feedback on the chapter about caring for the Earth and for checking our science. Thank you to all of the individuals, communities, and organizations whose justice stories offered inspiration in this book. We are grateful for your witness to the Holy.

Thank you to Brittany Sky McRay, Christy Lynch, the Rev. Sarah McWhirt-Toler, the Rev. Teresa Kim Pecinovsky, and the Rev. Dr. Lib Caldwell for your excitement and accompaniment through this process.

From Anita

To my family, thank you for your encouragement and affirmation, for instilling in me a sense of wonder, curiosity, and openness to experiencing God's grace. Scotty, thank you for your support and encouragement throughout this process, I love you.

Nanny, thank you for encouraging my creativity and for providing opportunities for me to explore and learn about environmental justice.

To all those who taught me in Sunday school at First United Methodist Church of Eaton Rapids: Carl and Marie Florian, Joyce Showerman, Doris Hall, and Elizabeth Scarlett, Mary Hofmann and my mama, thank you for being examples of compassionate Christian educators for me.

To my dear friends who encourage me to be my best self, to live creatively and curiously, to dance and sing and play and love with all I am: you know who you are, and I love you.

Thank you to my colleagues, Rev. Dr. Tim Phillips and Rev. Dr. Patricia L. Hunter, it is a gift to be in ministry together. And to the congregation of Seattle First Baptist Church, I love you, and I am so glad to be in ministry with all you young in age and young at heart.

To the youngest members of Seattle First Baptist Church and Glendale Baptist Church, thank you for all the shimmering moments, small and big, where you have shown me who God is and how to be in right relationship with each other and with the world. This book is because of you, and this book is for you.

Claire, thank you for inviting me into collaboration on this beautiful project. You inspire me and make me a better minister.

From Claire

Austin, thank you for holding my holy questions and cheering me on.

Sylvan and Amos: it's all for you, loves. May you wonder and grow in joyful compassion and make faith your own.

Thank you Jes Williams, Susan Sluser, and Mary Murphy, who showed me how to ask holy questions with kids in the catechesis atria.

Thank you to the Rev. Dr. Bonnie Miller-McLemore for teaching me to look for embodied theological knowing and the power of an open-ended question.

I give thanks to and for the parishes I've served during the creation of this project: St. Paul's Episcopal Chattanooga and St. Paul's Episcopal Athens. It's a gift to be part of the body of Christ here with you.

Anita, thank you for saying yes!

Printed in the USA
CPSIA information can be obtained
at www.ICGtesting.com
JSHW060042150824
68134JS00028B/2596

9 781640 654556